D0387477

MDTA

FOUNDATION OF FEDERAL MANPOWER POLICY

MDTA

FOUNDATION OF
FEDERAL MANPOWER POLICY

by Garth L. Mangum

The Johns Hopkins Press: Baltimore

Acknowledgments

THIS book is part of a continuing evaluation of federal manpower policies and programs financed by the Ford Foundation
at the Center for Manpower Policy Studies. Those to whom I
am indebted within the Departments of Labor and Health,
Education, and Welfare, and in the state employment services
and school systems are too numerous to name. The critical
comments of my colleagues Sar A. Levitan, Arnold L.
Nemore, and Lowell M. Glenn have resulted in important improvements.

GARTH L. MANGUM
The George Washington University

Contents

1:

Evaluating the Manpower
Development and Training Act

THE Manpower Development and Training Act of 1962 (MDTA) was the second (after the Area Redevelopment Act) of the New Frontier–Great Society anti-unemployment programs and the first to survive the rigors of economic and political experience. It is important both for its own sake and because it established a pattern which influenced the other manpower and antipoverty programs which followed.

THE MDTA EXPERIENCE

Although MDTA has to its credit numerous accomplishments which more than justify their cost, its original goal is not among them. The Act was passed primarily on the assumption that widespread job vacancies existed and that unemployment could be reduced by training the unemployed to fill them. Tens of thousands of persons trained under the Act are employed more steadily or have higher earnings than could have been expected if they had not participated in the program. The annual *Manpower Report of the President*, required by the Act, has raised manpower policy to a visibility and a status second only to fiscal and monetary policy in the hierarchy of economic policy-making. Federal, state, and local governments are engaged in various forms of manpower planning. MDTA's experimental and demonstration projects developed new tools for serving the disadvantaged, which were to become basic strategies in the "war against poverty." These innovations and

1

the earmarking of federal funds to such purposes have provided leverage to pressure lethargic institutions into serving population groups unfamiliar to them in new ways. The Act's research funds have uncovered new information and relationships, but, more important, they have played a major role in shifting the attention of academic labor economists from industrial relations to manpower problems. It is even possible that lower levels of unemployment may be achievable, with a given degree of price stability, than would have been the case without MDTA and related programs. However, there is no evidence that the unemployment rate is appreciably lower than it would have been had the program never existed.

This is no criticism of the program. The history of the Manpower Development and Training Act is an excellent illustration of the trial-and-error fashion in which the nation has entered the still highly experimental field of manpower policy. The Act was passed and amended by overwhelming bipartisan majorities in both houses of Congress and has enjoyed what has amounted to a legislative honeymoon experienced by few of the other manpower and antipoverty programs launched during the 1960's. Congress has been restrained in its expectations and willing to amend the program as experience demonstrated the need for amendment, and MDTA administrators have thus been relatively free to adapt to changing problems. The response of state and local governments, the public, and academic institutions to the program has been favorable. MDTA's early years have remained free from scandal and major criticism, except for the occasional charge that the program was "creaming"—training the most employable of the unemployed—rather than reaching out to attract those with serious disadvantages in competing for jobs.

MDTA has had its failures and successes, its unrealistic goals and its discoveries of the possible. Wrong decisions have been made, and right ones have been made too precipitously. Problems aplenty remain. Administrative procedures have moved slowly but deliberately toward decreased cumbersomeness. The administrators have been fairly honest with themselves and the public and have developed a data system which, though far from adequate, comes closer to providing the information needed for evaluation than does that of any similar program. MDTA's operations have been unspectacular, if not prosaic, but its accomplishments are solid and demonstrable.

EVALUATING SOCIAL PROGRAMS

The manpower development and training program (MDT), like all public programs, is financed from funds extracted from the nation's private citizens and private businesses through taxation and absorbs resources which could be used in other private or public activities. In allocating his income to one or another of the various consumption and investment alternatives available to him, the individual can make his own subjective judgments of the relative costs and benefits and can pursue, if not obtain, maximum satisfaction from his expenditures. The sum of individual decisions then determines the appropriate allocation of society's resources. No analogous system is available for measuring the relative costs and benefits of choices between the private and public sectors or within the public sector of the economy. In determining the level of public expenditures and choosing among programs, legislators can feel only at second hand, through the ballot, the pains and satisfactions of their constituents. The legislator and the administrator share responsibility in using public funds wisely, but what is the measure of that wisdom? As the role of government in the economy broadens and deepens, the generation of interest in and the development of techniques for the evaluation of public programs becomes crucial for economic efficiency and the welfare of society.

Recognition of this responsibility has led to the introduction of the Planning-Programming-Budgeting System (PPBS) throughout the federal government. The ambition of PPBS is to delineate objectives, examine alternatives, and identify the least-cost methods of achieving those objectives. The intent is admirable, but PPBS is still in its pioneering stage. At present it is focused on the operation of particular programs, with the intent of defining their goals and assuring consistency between goals and actions. Attainment of even these limited objectives is made difficult by the lack of consensus on objectives and the lack of data on program administration. PPBS cannot yet challenge the accomplishments of particular programs, let alone determine the relative effectiveness of those separately administered measures which pursue a common goal.

Simultaneously, academic economists, both because they recognize that manpower, poverty, and other social welfare programs are here to stay and because research funds have been available for the purpose, have begun applying to manpower programs cost-benefit analysis techniques formerly restricted to the areas of defense spending and development of natural resources. However, cost-benefit analysis has greater potential than current value as an evaluation technique. No federal manpower program now has a reporting system capable of producing data of the kind needed for adequate evaluation. Even the data available are rarely subjected to careful analysis. In addition, many of the benefits and some of the costs are nonquantifiable, leaving to assumption and judgment broad areas of assessment. For example, to incorporate into the mainstream of society an otherwise alienated individual or group may have social value far beyond the potential contributions to earnings or to the gross national product. On the other hand, to create benefits in excess of costs is only a necessary, not a sufficient, justification for expenditure of public funds. There may be more efficient ways of reaching the same objectives, and these must be examined to assure use of the least costly approach. More basic may be a lack of clear objectives or pursuit of low-priority objectives. Costs and benefits cannot be compared until it is clear what can be counted as a benefit. These technical problems, while they do not challenge the conceptual validity of cost-benefit analysis, do raise questions of its current usefulness. They also lead to conflicting and inconclusive results which allow those with vested interests to insert their bias into supposedly objective findings.

Finally, all public expenditures that result in benefits in excess of direct costs are not automatically justified. The opportunity costs—the value of the other activities which private taxpayers or other public users might have undertaken with the same resources—must also be considered. Priorities between the private and public sectors and among public uses are established through the political process. Adequate evaluation requires determination that the appropriated resources are being used to pursue the politically defined objectives.

This evaluation of the manpower development and training program faced many handicaps. The MDTA data reporting system, although inadequate, for evaluation purposes is so far superior to that of any other manpower or antipoverty program that one is more inclined to praise it than to complain about it. Other programs have been launched in haste, with much attention given to delivering services and disbursing funds and little concern for building organizational capability and for evaluating results. Financial controls may vary from loose to tight, but data for evaluation is always an afterthought, all too often collected for the sake of public relations rather than decision-making. In such company, MDTA looks good.

MDTA had the advantage of being launched by an agency with long experience in data gathering and analysis. Basic reporting forms, therefore, were developed almost automatically, but little thought was given to defining objectives and assuring the proper analysis and evaluation of the data thus collected. The result is a reporting system which can provide most of the current and historical information needed for evaluating the results of the program, but it lacks the capacity to provide information needed for day-to-day program management. The system cannot offer completeness of reporting or assurance of accuracy. It has suffered from inadequate staff and from lack of the top-level interest which would assure that the data emerged from the computers, were analyzed, and were published. Fortunately, MDTA data have escaped the fate of many statistics in that they have not been deliberately used to confuse. They have suffered from disuse rather than misuse.

The data used in this study represent extensive efforts by officials and technicians of the Department of Labor and of Health, Education, and Welfare, in response to a congressional request. A mass of data, much of which had been hidden away on computer tapes, emerged, but they all suffered from the same basic limitations. The accuracy with which forms were filled out at the local and state levels had not been checked. The data provided almost complete coverage on the characteristics of trainees, and information on hourly earnings and employment history immediately prior to enrollment in the program was provided, but the time period covered was not sufficient to serve as a dependable base line for comparison with post-training employment and income. Post-training experience was seriously under-reported: information was available on 56 percent of those trained in educational institutions and on only 38 percent of those trained on the job. Detailed demographic characteristics were available for only 34 percent of those who completed institutional training and for only 16 percent of those who completed on-the-job training. No follow-up beyond the first year was available. Because there appeared to be no obvious biases in the under-reporting, the data were accepted at face value, yet their limitations were kept in mind.

MDTA financial data pose particular problems. A system

has been carefully constructed to assure that the taxpayer's dollars are not lost or stolen, but the system makes it extraordinarily difficult to tie expenditures and costs to program enrollments and completions. An increasing awareness of the shortcomings of the data system is apparent. Program administrators are becoming more aware of the dangers of "blind flying" and "seat-of-the-pants" decision-making. Management information rather than evaluation is the focus of current concern, but if information is made available for management purposes, many of the obstacles to evaluation will also be eliminated. Thus, there is reason to hope that the MDTA reporting system will be developed into a model for other programs, as well as an aid to decision-makers and a boon to future evaluators.

The remaining obstacles to evaluation of MDTA require less wordy caveats. There is no merit in attempting to quantify the nonquantifiable. One can only identify, describe, and exercise his judgment without apology. An examination of alternative solutions to the problems that MDTA tackled is beyond the scope of this book. That more effective alternatives can be designed is likely but not currently verifiable. Evaluation of other programs designed for similar objectives and clientele has failed to identify more effective alternatives.[1] That prevention rather than remediation of present problems would have proved cheaper is likely, but we must start from where we are to attack problems as they exist.

The generally accepted approach to program evaluation is to identify program objectives, then to assess the degree to which those objectives have been attained, the efficiency shown in attempting to attain them, and the cost of the attempt. The political process within which public programs are

---

[1] See, for instance, Sar A. Levitan, *Antipoverty Work and Training Efforts: Goals and Reality*, The Institute of Labor and Industrial Relations, University of Michigan, Policy Paper No. 3 (Ann Arbor, Mich.: By the Institute, 1967).

developed is not that orderly, however. Only rarely are objectives clearly defined. Experience often exposes the unreality of the original assumptions. Economic and other conditions are subject to continual and sometimes radical changes. As such changes occur, programs are revised, sometimes explicitly by amendment, but more often by administrative practice. In some cases program objectives and reality never mesh, though more often, given time, programs either develop a suitable function or, in rare cases, disappear.

OBJECTIVES

This book has two objectives: (1) to trace the policy-making processes by which MDTA has taken on its present shape, and (2) to evaluate as objectively as possible the successes and failures, benefits and shortcomings, of the Manpower Development and Training Act. Chapter 2 traces the legislative history of the Act. Chapter 3 follows the administrative developments by which legislative authorization and appropriation became an operating program. Chapter 4 compares the contributions and costs of the training program for the unemployed which is the heart of the Act, and Chapter 5 describes and analyzes the impact of the research, experimental, and manpower-planning aspects of the MDTA experience. The final chapter explores some continuing basic issues, the resolution of which will determine the future role of MDTA in the nation's manpower policies.

2:

Legislative Evolution

MDTA's legislative honeymoon began because it so neatly bridged a series of debates in 1961 both within the new Kennedy Administration and between the Administration and its opponents. Immediately following the inauguration, the third post-Korean recession struck bottom, with unemployment rising to above 7 percent. Unemployment had drifted persistently upward during the 1950's, reaching a higher point in each recession and retaining a higher residual during each recovery. It was not only high among inexperienced youths and minority groups but reached 5 percent for married men as well. Although each explanation offered led to a different policy recommendation, all observers seemed to agree on the need for a federal retraining program.

ANTECEDENTS

To the new breed of Keynesian macroeconomists who had recently joined the Council of Economic Advisers, the answer was straightforward—increase aggregate demand through general fiscal and monetary policy. Labor market specialists, both in the Labor Department and the universities, impressed by the concentration of unemployment by age, race, skill, education, and geography, recommended direct attacks on the structural problems. For senators and congressmen, concerned with particular constituents in particular communities, the structural explanation struck a responsive chord. Increasing numbers of people in all walks of life were beginning to see automation as a growing menace that was destroying the skills

9

of mature, experienced workers. Fiscal conservatives, including the chairman of the Federal Reserve Board, an ex-chairman of the Council of Economic Advisers, and various congressmen and senators, anxious to restrain spending and balance budgets, were convinced that there was no shortage of jobs. To them, the fault was in the unemployed who lacked the appropriate education or skills, were located in the wrong places and immobile, or who didn't really want to work.

Retraining offered something attractive to everyone. To the structuralist and the fiscal conservative, it was a frontal attack on the problem. To the concerned legislator, it represented direct aid to his constituents. The expansionist, while convinced that training would not create jobs, acknowledged that some mismatches between available skills and job vacancies were likely and welcomed the expenditure on retraining as a addition to total demand.

THE AREA REDEVELOPMENT ACT

Training proposals also had the advantage of substantial exposure in the legislature. S. 1 in the new Congress was the Area Redevelopment Act, sponsored by Senator Paul Douglas, which had been thoroughly debated and vetoed twice since 1955.[1] Senator Douglas' purpose was to provide employers with federal incentives to locate or expand in depressed areas. One of the bill's key provisions was a program to retrain the unemployed, thus offering a ready-made work force to a newly arrived employer. Since no one could be against training, the issues were federal involvement, the need for financial assistance to trainees, and the respective roles of the Department of Labor and the Department of Health, Education, and Welfare and their local affiliates. The first two of these issues had been

[1] Sar A. Levitan, *Federal Aid to Depressed Areas: An Evaluation of the Area Redevelopment Administration* (Baltimore: The Johns Hopkins Press, 1964).

debated in the Congress and within the previous Administration and had been resolved, at least in general, before MDTA arrived on the scene.

The official position of the Eisenhower Administration on the depressed areas legislation was dominated by the Council of Economic Advisers: training and retraining were good, but the responsibility was a private or state and local one. Only the Department of Labor took a serious interest in the pros and cons of a federal training program. The political appointees within the Department initially endorsed the Administration's opinion but are reported to have become converted to the cause of training and to have unsuccessfully advocated a training program in Cabinet meetings toward the close of the Administration's tenure. The career civil servants in the Department were also divided to some degree, but only as to the strength of their commitment.

A crucial element in the retraining proposal was the provision of some form of subsistence payments for unemployed heads of families during training, and most proposals involved some degree of attachment to the unemployment insurance system. The Administration response had been to indicate that the sanctity of the payroll-tax-based system should not be violated and that it was up to the states to determine whether an eligible unemployed person in training was available for work as required by law. Therefore, Labor Department staff members ranged from enthusiastic advocates to more cautious persons who shared the official concern for the unemployment compensation implications of the proposals.

Within the Department of Labor the conviction was general that vocational education was too far out of touch with the world of work to be useful. Those outside the federal agency providing vocational education funds seemed to agree. Early versions of the Douglas bill would have given the Secretary of Labor authority to determine training needs and to contract with local schools for the training. However, through the inter-

vention of the American Vocational Association (AVA),
later versions divided these responsibilities between the Secretary of Labor and the Secretary of Health, Education, and
Welfare, even though the latter's agency had shown little interest in the discussion. Congressional debates involved the same
issues, and added the fear that the federal purse was being
opened to claims of uncertain magnitude.

THE SPECIAL COMMITTEE ON UNEMPLOYMENT PROBLEMS

By 1961 these issues had been largely resolved, and the
depressed areas bill awaited only executive acceptance. Meanwhile, bipartisan support had been developing for a broader
training bill not restricted to depressed areas. In 1959, to ful-
fill a commitment made to an AFL-CIO "Unemployment
March on Washington," the then Majority Leader of the Senate, Lyndon B. Johnson, appointed a Special Committee on
Unemployment Problems under the chairmanship of Senator
Eugene J. McCarthy. In field hearings, employers complained
of job vacancies and no skilled help, while the unemployed, as
often as not, attributed their hardships to technological displacement.

Retraining the unemployed seemed a logical answer, and
vocational education appeared to be the appropriate vehicle.
However, it was apparent from testimony that adult workers
could not undertake training without financial support. A
number of key senators were particularly disturbed to find
that, in most states, if an unemployed person entered a training program, he was considered unavailable for work and
therefore ineligible for unemployment insurance benefits.

Administration reluctance to add subsistence allowances to
the burdens of the unemployment compensation system per-
sisted, but congressional opinion was more liberal. Both the
majority and minority reports of the Special Committee on

Unemployment Problems recommended expansion of federal support for vocational education with subsistence payments to adult trainees.[2] However, the minority report was more forthright on the subsistence issue. With staff support from the knowledgeable and by then firmly committed Labor Department, the Republicans advocated a special federal fund from which to pay training allowances equal to, but separate from, unemployment insurance.

Giving legislative reality to the McCarthy committee's training recommendations became the task of the new Subcommittee on Employment and Manpower, established in the Committee on Labor and Public Welfare in fulfillment of another recommendation. Because Senator Jennings Randolph of West Virginia, the second ranking Democrat on the new subcommittee, was campaigning for re-election, he assumed the chairmanship temporarily. However, the ranking member, Senator Joseph S. Clark of Pennsylvania, was slated to take over after the election, assuming continued Democratic control, and the primary task of developing a retraining bill was his.

The State of Pennsylvania had a small, underfinanced program to retrain unemployed adults in its vocational schools as part of its efforts at industrial development. At Clark's request a bill was drafted in early 1960 by vocational educators from Pennsylvania and AVA, calling for a federal program of a similar nature. Essentially, the proposal was to add an additional grant-in-aid category to the Smith-Hughes Vocational Education Act authorizing retraining of the adult unemployed.

Clark's personal interest in manpower led him in other directions, however. A former air force officer and mayor of Philadelphia, he was experienced in deploying military personnel, recruiting high-talent manpower, and allocating and

---

[2] U.S., Congress, Senate, Special Committee on Unemployment Problems, *S. Report No. 1206*, 86th Cong., 2d sess., 1960, pp. 124, 186.

directing staff.[3] His phrase for it was "staffing freedom," and the notion was the essence of his S. 3555, introduced in the Senate in May, 1960. Its intent was to exalt manpower considerations in the schema of economic policy-making by establishing a Council of Manpower Advisers, analogous to the Council of Economic Advisers, and by requiring an annual *Manpower Report of the President,* analogous to the President's *Economic Report.* The retraining bill was introduced as S. 3760 by Senator Randolph, who held field hearings on it in his home state of West Virginia.

AGREEING ON A TRAINING BILL

With the 1960 election past, Clark sought out the President-elect to solicit support for his manpower policy proposal, but he was thwarted by Mr. Kennedy's advisers, who counseled that having an employment-oriented economist among the members of the Council of Economic Advisers would be sufficient. With that rebuff, Clark turned his mind to the retraining bill and reintroduced it as S. 987 in February, 1961.

Compromising Competing Interests

S. 987 soon found itself in the middle of a bureaucratic dispute of considerable consequence. The bill simply proposed adding another category to the Smith-Hughes Act of 1917 to provide federal grants-in-aid for training those who are unemployed as a result of "structural changes," but it also added training allowances for those ineligible for unemployment compensation. Priority was to be given to heads of households over thirty years of age with at least five years of labor market experience.

Despite its origin in and attachment to vocational education,

---

[3] See his Introduction to *The Annals of the American Academy of Political and Social Science,* "American Civilization and Its Leadership Needs, 1960–1990," No. 325 (September, 1959).

the Office of Education showed little interest in the bill, but the officers of the American Vocational Association were strongly committed to its passage. However, the system of vocational education was in disrepute, and one of the new president's early acts was to appoint a panel to study it and make recommendations for its revitalization.[4] Until that was done there was reluctance to rely on the existing institutional machinery or add to its burdens. On the other hand, in his early West Virginia campaigning President Kennedy had become an advocate of retraining and had mentioned the proposal in a number of speeches, yet the Administration had not followed up the campaign commitment with any concrete proposal.

In reacting to the Clark retraining proposal, staff members of the Bureau of the Budget, remembering with favor the direct relationship between the Veterans Administration and the schools under the G.I. Bill, advocated a similar approach to retraining. They proposed that the local employment services identify needs, promote on-the-job training, and contract with local public and private schools for institutional training. The Labor Department staff was divided between those willing to compromise for AVA support and those who stood with the Bureau of the Budget. In an internal memorandum to the new Secretary of Labor, Arthur Goldberg, the latter group expressed the view that "retraining can best be supplied by industry and not through the archaic vocational education system." They maintained that the funding increases for vocational education contemplated by the Clark bill would "so consolidate the power of the American Vocational Association that little hope would remain for elimination of a part of the educational system completely at variance with national objectives and the current needs of the economy." However, rather than risk a direct confrontation with the AVA, it was

[4] Panel of Consultants on Vocational Education, *Education for a Changing World of Work* (Washington, D.C.: U.S. Government Printing Office, 1962).

decided to endorse the Clark bill provisionally while seeking the Senator's commitment to a broader program.

Testimony was therefore prepared for Goldberg praising Clark and endorsing the bill but stressing the need for a more comprehensive approach to all manpower programs; encompassing counseling, placement, relocation, job creation, and general education, in addition to training. The latter would include on-the-job training as well as training in vocational institutions. Goldberg had been assigned by the President to develop such a program, the testimony said, and therefore the Administration was urging postponement of consideration of S. 987. The Goldberg testimony had been scheduled for April 10, 1961, but the hearing was canceled and a breakfast meeting was arranged between Goldberg and Clark. Goldberg proposed that Clark's original S. 3555 be incorporated with S. 987 but with the Secretary of Labor as Manpower Adviser to the President, in the place of Clark's Council of Manpower Advisers.

The Senate subcommittee staff was fully aware of the strength of the American Vocational Association and knew that any training bill which lacked its support had no chance of passage. The Labor Department was now willing to compromise to gain the needed support, but the Budget Bureau staff remained adamant. The Administration bill, S. 1991, sent to Congress on May 29, 1961, placed the Secretary of Labor in control and authorized full federal financing rather than matching grants. Though providing for the use of state vocational education facilities as well as on-the-job training, it did so through individual project-by-project agreements, to be negotiated by the Secretary of Health, Education, and Welfare, rather than through allocation of funds to the states by formula. The training program was Title II of the bill. Title I, which Secretary Goldberg and Senator Clark read as assigning the former a special role as Manpower Adviser to the President, was actually a melding of the manpower report portion

of the Senator's proposal with one endorsing a research program, written by Labor Department technicians.

The bill had to have support for passage, however, and
when the AVA presented demands for thirty-four amendments to the Clark subcommittee, twenty of them were accepted. To these were added a few more that were demanded
by Republican members of the subcommittee. The role of
HEW was strengthened. After the second year 50 percent
state financial participation was to be required. Training allowances were limited to heads of families with three years'
experience in the labor force, though an opening was left for
the Secretary of Labor to authorize allowances for youths
under special circumstances. The subcommittee not only deleted the Administration's proposal for underwriting the costs
of relocating the unemployed but specified that the training
provided could not assist the relocation of an employer. It
gave priority to training for jobs within a state, inserted a formula for allocation of funds among the states, and assigned
any equipment purchased to the state, though forbidding the
use of MDTA funds for construction of buildings. The subcommittee bill also established a National Manpower Advisory Committee with membership drawn from labor, management, and the public, and encouraged, but did not require, the
establishment of state and local advisory committees to help
determine the appropriateness of training activities in their
communities.

Senate Passage

Not a single opponent rose to speak against the bill on the
Senate floor. Senator Winston L. Prouty of Vermont, a subcommittee member and strong advocate of the legislation,
proposed amendments to reduce the Act's duration from four
to two years and to eliminate the provision authorizing payment of training allowances to youths under special circumstances. Senator Clark had limited his 1960 bill and the sub-

committee bill to experienced adults because he judged that his political support would not extend to youths and marginal workers. Senator Prouty believed that the program should be limited to the experienced worker with family responsibilities whose skills had been made obsolete by technological change, leaving the problems of new labor force entrants to the schools and the pending Youth Employment Act. His advocacy of a shortened duration reflected not opposition to the program but a cautious preference for an early congressional review of the experience. A few of the 30 senators who subsequently voted against the bill spoke for the Prouty amendments but gave no more general opposition. The bill was amended to limit youths between sixteen and twenty-two years of age to no more than 5 percent of total training allowance expenditures. The limitation to two years lost by a single vote, while the amended bill was approved 60–31.

House Passage

The House played a limited role in the formulation of the Act. The Select Subcommittee on Labor of the Committee on Education and Labor was involved in hearings delving into the impact of automation on employment. It adopted the Administration bill with few changes, deleting the relocation proposal and adding an apportionment formula. Lacking AVA support, the bill was stuck in the House Rules Committee when Congress adjourned.

A head count the following January suggested 150 to 160 sure votes with the possibility of an additional 30 southern supporters. It was clear that at least 30 Republican votes would be needed. The American Vocational Association could help swing a favorable southern vote, but the support of moderate Republicans had to be won. Probing disclosed that Congressman Charles E. Goodell of New York, who was the key to moderate Republican support, would not accept the

Administration bill but was willing to support the Senate bill. When internal subcommittee efforts at compromise failed, Congressman Goodell introduced what was essentially the Senate bill. Then, when it became apparent in floor debate that sufficient votes were lacking, the House subcommittee chairman, Congressman Elmer J. Holland, introduced an amendment substituting the text of the Goodell bill but bearing his own name and bill number. This bipartisan product the House endorsed 354–62.

The heart of the new legislation was full federal financing for the first two years, followed by continued full federal support for on-the-job training but providing only 50 percent matching funds for institutional training of the unemployed in occupations for which there were reasonable expectations of employment. Heads of families with at least three years of labor market experience or heads of farm families with annual incomes below $1,200 could qualify for up to fifty-two weeks of training allowances at levels equal to the average unemployment compensation benefit in the state. Limited numbers of youths aged nineteen to twenty-one years, inclusive, could receive training allowances of $20 a week. Title I, with its requirement for an annual *Manpower Report* by the President and its authorization for research, was included but passed almost completely without comment.

THE 1963 AMENDMENTS

Subsequent reviews and amendments of MDTA have been marked by the same bipartisan authorship and support that were evident at the birth of the program. Without the need for defensiveness, it has been possible for the Act's administrators and congressional supporters to admit shortcomings, to request and obtain improvements, and to adapt the program to changing labor market conditions.

Developing Issues

When conceived in 1960–1961, with general unemployment averaging above 6 percent and with 5 percent of married men seeking jobs, the Act was apparently viewed by most members of Congress as a temporary recession expedient to aid the displaced experienced worker. The Act was signed on March 15, 1962, but money was not appropriated until the end of August. By that time, though the general level of unemployment had declined only to 5.7 percent (seasonally adjusted), the rate for married men had fallen to 3.7 percent. By July, 1963, the unemployment rate for the latter was down to 3.2 percent, though the overall rate had hardly changed. The offsetting factor was a rise in teenage unemployment. Most of the experienced heads of families with "obsolete" skills were either back at their old jobs or were learning new ones at their employer's expense. Public concern was focused again on the 16 to 18 percent unemployment rates of teenagers, characterized by Dr. James B. Conant and others as "social dynamite."[5] Meanwhile, the Youth Employment bill, first introduced by Senator Hubert H. Humphrey in the late 1950's and passed by the Senate in 1959 and 1963 had been bottled up in the House Rules Committee.[6] Despite the limitation on training allowances for those aged nineteen through twenty-one years, youths under twenty-two (including those aged sixteen to eighteen who could be trained without allowances), who comprised 28 percent of all the unemployed, comprised almost one-quarter of the trainees in the first fiscal year.

With the late start, only 30,000 trainees were enrolled in fiscal 1963, in contrast to the projected 65,000. Not only had appropriations been delayed, but the task turned out to be more difficult than anticipated. Regulations had to be written; projects negotiated, approved, and funded; facilities, equip-

---

[5] National Committee for Children and Youth, *Social Dynamite* (Washington, D.C.: By the Committee, 1961).

[6] Levitan, *Antipoverty Work and Training Efforts*, p. 6.

ment, and instructors obtained; trainees recruited; and training begun. In addition, what had been designed as a retraining program for those with obsolete skills was being changed by economic recovery to a training program for those who had never been skilled. To obtain the 30,000 enrollees over 150,-000 persons had been tested and screened.[7] The characteristics of the trainees matched those of all the unemployed by race and length of unemployment, but older workers and those with little education were grossly under-represented.

Rather than being a temporary phenomenon related to the initiation of the training program, however, the under-representation proved to be a continuing source of concern and criticism which is still not satisfactorily solved. The major institutions involved had a tendency toward "creaming" built into their methodology, where it was more difficult to root out than would have been the case had it been limited to their preferences. The state employment services were accustomed to matching employer job orders with the most capable workers available, and they were quite capable of referring to training projects only those who came seeking unemployment compensation or job referrals. There were neither the resources nor the experience for "outreach" to ferret out those who needed such services worst but who tended to seek them least. Vocational educators were not only representatives of the school systems that many of the undereducated had rejected but their teaching and training methods assumed a reasonable amount of basic education. The Bureau of Apprenticeship and Training staff which administered the on-the-job training portion of MDTA was accustomed to promoting apprenticeship, leaving it up to the employers and unions to find and select the apprentices.

The manpower development and training (MDT) program

---

[7] U.S., Congress, Senate, Committee on Labor and Public Welfare, Subcommittee on Employment and Manpower, *Nation's Manpower Revolution*, 88th Cong., 1st sess., 1963, pt. 2:400.

was in no danger of faltering for lack of trainable persons.[8] Even with an improving job market, reasonably attractive trainees were available. However, with rising employment they were becoming a progressively smaller portion relative to the disadvantaged groups, who were becoming more visible and were a subject for increased concern.

Disturbed at the "creaming" propensity of the employment services and public schools, federal MDTA administrators had launched their own "experimental and demonstration" projects. These bypassed the states, giving direct federal support primarily to private, nonprofit, community-based organizations serving various disadvantaged groups but with an accent upon youth. The experimental and demonstration projects and the regular MDT projects were all presenting the same message: literacy was a prerequisite of known methods of occupational training. Nothing in the Act forbade provision of basic education. A few states had interpreted the law liberally to allow a basic education component in MDT courses, but other states and some federal officials were more doubtful.[9]

There were other problems. Average training allowances of $35 per week were proving inadequate for heads of families, who were often forced to drop out of the program to take short-term jobs when completion would mean improved chances of more favorable long-term employment. The "reasonable expectation of employment" requirement was being interpreted too restrictively. In a few cases, apparently, employers had even been asked for written promises that they would hire trainees upon completion of their courses. It was more common, however, for current job openings to be considered necessary for initiation of training, to be completed several weeks or months in the future.[10]

---

[8] The initials MDT are used in reference to the Title II training program, in contrast to MDTA, which refers to the entire Act or its administration.

[9] *Nation's Manpower Revolution*, pt. 2:495, 531.

[10] *Ibid.*, p. 536.

The most immediate of all problems was budgetary, however. The first of the two years of full federal financing had passed, and in another year the federal component would decline to the 50 percent ratio customary for support of vocational education. Most of the state legislatures had met at the beginning of 1963, when the program was almost unknown. Thirty-six states had not even requested funds, and only three had made token appropriations. When polled by the American Vocational Association, thirty-four states replied they would be unable to participate after June 30, 1964, unless 100 percent federal financing continued. Only six states could assure matching appropriations. New project proposals were already drying up by the summer of 1963 because no project could be funded which contemplated training extending beyond June 30, 1964.[11] State officials and vocational educators had many complaints about the particulars of administrative practices, but they were wholeheartedly for continuation of the program. However, they were doubtful whether it stood high enough in priority with their governors and legislators to survive without continued federal funding.

Developing the Amendments

The Senate had led while the House followed in the development and passage of MDTA in 1962, but in 1963 the leadership moved to the House side. The Senate subcommittee was involved in an extensive exploration of a wide range of manpower problems and would have preferred to minimize the 1963 amendments, awaiting further experience and completion of its studies before proposing more extensive changes. Reflecting that strategy, the Senate proposals were limited to expansion of the portion of the program dealing with youth,

---

[11] U.S., Congress, Senate, Committee on Labor and Public Welfare, Subcommittee on Employment and Manpower, *Manpower Retraining, Hearings on S. 1691, S. 1716, S. 1725, S. 1831,* 88th Cong., 1st sess., July 16, 18, 1963, pp. 12–14.

extending the allowance period to make possible inclusion of "literacy and basic work skills," and providing full federal financing for an additional grace year.

The House subcommittee had more ambitious plans, and the senators fell in line by adopting the House version. Representatives of organized labor in particular were pressing for less local orientation, the addition of relocation assistance, more generous training allowances, and compulsory establishment of local manpower advisory committees, as well as the changes sought by the Senate. The establishment of the committees was an indirect approach to attacking one of labor's major criticisms of the Act. Unions complained that MDT projects were interfering in apprenticeable trades, providing people with skills already available among unemployed persons who could be relocated, and allowing employers to establish excessive qualifications for acceptance of trainees.[12] Union representation on local manpower advisory committees could provide some protection against these evils. However, such committees were not required under the original Act even though the National Manpower Advisory Committee had the assignment to "encourage and assist" their establishment. The national committee had no local machinery for doing so and left the responsibility to the local employment services, who also had no strong motivation to do so.

The House subcommittee developed a bill extending the Act until 1967, with full federal financing continuing through fiscal 1965, followed by two-thirds financing in fiscal 1966, and 50 percent financing in fiscal 1967. Training allowances were authorized for up to twenty weeks of basic education, making a total potential training period of seventy-two weeks. The youth portion of the program was expanded to a maximum of 25 percent of the trainees receiving allowances, in-

---

[12] *Ibid.*, pp. 73–74, and U.S., Congress, House, Committee on Education and Labor, Select Subcommittee on Labor, *Hearings on H.R. 6991, H.R. 7000 and H.R. 7377*, 88th Cong., 1st sess. 1963, p. 379.

cluding those aged seventeen years or more who had been out of school for one year. The latter requirement reflected continued concern that training allowances might provide an incentive for dropping out of school. At the same time the three-year labor force attachment requirement was reduced to two years and a person other than the head of the household was made eligible to receive training allowances if the family head were unemployed. Finally, allowances were liberalized by the addition of $10 per week above the unemployment compensation level, and provision was made to allow institutional trainees to work twenty hours a week without a reduction in their allowances.

Authority and initiative for establishing local manpower advisory committees was transferred to the Secretary of Labor. To counter the claims of training institutions that they had been bypassed in favor of public institutions, the provision allowing states to use private institutions where public facilities were inadequate was changed to direct their use whenever they could provide equivalent training at lower cost.

The relocation proposal in the 1962 Administration bill had been killed primarily by merchants from depressed areas who complained they would rather have customers with welfare checks than no customers at all.[13] An out-and-out relocation program was not yet politically salable, but a "foot in the door" was achieved. The Secretary of Labor was authorized to use up to $4 million of Title II appropriations for grants and loans to cover relocation expenses in pilot projects designed to test the effectiveness of subsidized geographical mobility as a weapon against unemployment.

Bipartisanship was evident at all stages in both houses, and a number of the liberalizations were proposed by Republicans. The Senate committee unanimously supported the bill, and 8 of 13 Republican members of the House committee endorsed

[13] *Ibid.*, p. 523.

the favorable report. On the floors of both the Senate and the House the only criticisms were directed at the cost and possible duplication of the Vocational Education Act of 1963. The amendments passed the Senate in September by a vote of 76–8. The House Republicans made a show of economy by attempting to cut $270 million from the bill's four-year authorization. Yet when Representative Sam Gibbons of Florida out-economized them by proposing a $280 million cut, simply by deleting the final year, the amended bill still passed on a voice vote by 392–0. MDTA had taken a significant step away from being a temporary recession measure to aid the readjustment of displaced skilled workers toward becoming a permanent remedial program to alleviate serious inequalities in the competition for jobs.

THE 1965 AMENDMENTS

The 1965 amendments were initiated by the Labor Department but in the end also bore the stamp of the minority members of the Senate Subcommittee on Employment and Manpower. Both Senate and House hearings were even more of a "love-in" than in 1963. There were no basic criticisms of the program from either witnesses or minority members, although, in a few cases, the former thought the groups they represented were not getting enough attention. The amendments proposed by the latter were entirely positive and were in some cases more generous than the proposals of the majority. The same vocational educators who had criticized administrative complexities in 1963 had nothing but praise in 1965. In the end, Congress extended the Act to 1969 rather than making it permanent, as the Administration had requested. The committees made it clear that the continuance was assumed, but that they desired the opportunity for periodic review.

Changing Matching Requirements

The most immediate concern was unchanged from 1963: how to move the program toward the permanent federal financing which the Administration had originally proposed. The 1963 reprieve was near its end, and on July 1, 1965, the states would have to put up one-third of the money. Although wholehearted in their praise for the program the states protested their inability to pay for it. The Administration countered with a 90:10 compromise, using the interstate highway program as an analogy. The subcommittees in both the House and Senate were disposed to be more generous. The House Select Subcommittee on Labor amended the bill to continue full federal financing, but the full Committee on Education and Labor preferred another compromise. They opted for full federal funding of training allowances and 90 percent financing of training costs, with the states' 10 percent provided in cash or "in kind."

Senator Clark was the defender of the Administration proposal. Though his original limitation of the program to adults was a matter of political strategy, his commitment to state financial participation was real. During debate on the 1963 amendments he had strongly urged that the states be given one more year of full federal financing and then, if they did not pick up their share, that the program should be allowed to die. His endorsing the Administration position was a major concession.

In the Senate, it was the united minority of Senators Jacob K. Javits, Winston L. Prouty, and George L. Murphy which introduced and pushed hardest for the House position.[14] The national nature of the causes of unemployment, the mobility of labor, and the practicality of establishing manpower training centers serving market areas overlapping state lines were

[14] U.S., Congress, Senate, Committee on Labor and Public Welfare, *S. Rept. No. 123*, 89th Cong., 1st sess., March, 1965, pp. 33, 36.

all arguments for federal support. The complaint of private schools that matching requirements would interfere with their ambitions for a larger role brought a special exemption allowing full funding of training costs for private institutions as well as for on-the-job training.

Training Allowances

Bipartisan support was given to an additional allowance of $5 per dependent to a maximum of $20 per week. Other evidences of bipartisan generosity were the provision of training allowances to single persons living alone and to more than one member of a family in which the head of the household was unemployed, as well as the extension of part-time working privileges to on-the-job trainees.

Refresher Courses for Professionals

Despite the 1963 extension of the training period to 72 weeks to cover the addition of basic education, only 1 percent of all MDT projects were funded for longer than 52 weeks in 1964, the same percentage as in the previous year. Yet the Administration proposed extension of funding to 104 weeks to make possible inclusion of training of technicians. Senator Javits sought specifically to include professional employees, reflecting his view that MDTA's goals included meeting manpower needs as well as employing the unemployed. Congress did not overrule the administrative decision to forbid professional training, but it was made clear that "refresher" courses for professionals, particularly those displaced by defense contract cancellations and military base closings, were in order.

The Role of Research, Experimentation, and Demonstration

Two significant changes were made in Title I of the Act, reflecting apparent congressional approval of the research and experimental and demonstration activities. Congress never seriously discussed in hearings, reports, or floor debate the ob-

jectives of the MDTA research program, but administrative
practice had limited its use to contracts for direct program-
and policy-related topics. The 1965 amendments specifically
added grant authority.

The Experimental and Demonstration (E & D) program
had been undertaken by means of a liberal interpretation of
somewhat vague language rather than by specific authorization. These activities were of necessity undertaken with Title
II funds which were subject to the state allocation formula.
Thus, though E & D projects were federally promoted and
supervised, it was necessary either to obtain state agreement
on their use of allocated funds or to rely upon funds not
utilized by the states. The impending 10 percent state matching requirement would have complicated matters further. Not
only the state employment services and vocational educators
but their federal counterparts had opposed the E & D expenditures, arguing that they could use the money more effectively
and in a more orderly fashion. The House subcommittee had
defended the E & D effort in its 1963 report but had adopted
no formal amendment.

The 1965 amendments further endorsed the E & D program
by explicitly including it in Title I, where it could receive its
own appropriation unencumbered by state matching or allocation formulas. As part of this E & D authority the bill increased funds for the Labor Mobility Demonstration Project
from $4 to $5 million, extended it through 1967, and gave
the Secretary of Labor greater discretion in providing assistance. In addition, the Secretary was authorized to undertake
another special project, using $200,000 the first year and
$300,000 the second year, to provide bonding for those whose
police records were an impediment to employment.

State Funding Relationships
The 1963 hearings had resounded with complaints from the
states on delays in funding and renewing projects. These were

muted in 1965, but an amendment proposed by Senator Javits was adopted delegating to the states review and approval of institutional projects costing less than $75,000. A related and more important Javits amendment restricted federal authority to reapportion funds among the states.

The original Act provided a formula for allocation of Title II funds but allowed administrative reapportionment from states which had not committed all of their apportionment to states needing additional funds. In the first year only a few states were ready to move rapidly with the program. Though the Act was adopted in March, no funds were appropriated until August, and then only $70 million of an authorized $100 million was approved. Only eighteen states committed their full share, and they were given added funds from the uncommitted portions. Some remaining funds were earmarked for fiscal 1964 to pay allowances to trainees enrolled in fiscal 1963 programs which extended into the following year. Even then, seventeen states did not use their full apportionment, while others were unable to fund all their training proposals (see Table 2-1). Those states which received more than their allocated share created a larger capability and a built-in voracious appetite for the next year.

In fiscal 1964, the program operated on continuing resolutions for three and a half months before funds were appropriated in October, 1963. Although the Labor Department had requested the full authorization of $165 million, Congress appropriated only $110 million, instructing the Department to commit it as rapidly as possible, returning for supplemental funds if needed. Several states had already committed their full share of the smaller appropriation by that time. The Labor Department thereupon allocated the remaining funds so as to give those states more than their apportionment and the others less, but, even so, 86 percent of the appropriated funds was exhausted by December 31, 1963. A supplemental amount of $55 million was requested, and the remaining funds were se-

Table 2-1

*Project Funding Approvals as a Percent of Amount Available
in Accordance with Apportionment*

State or Possession	Fiscal Year				
	1963	1964	1965	1966	1967[a]
Alabama	74	325	65	121	70
Alaska	234	1,176	103	70	57
Arizona	162	185	171	142	46
Arkansas	100	67	45	88	67
California	84	84	87	90	59
Colorado	127	114	146	103	54
Connecticut	90	150	83	115	36
Delaware	15	232	62	105	58
District of Columbia	236	452	233	165	138
Florida	53	108	77	115	66
Georgia	54	262	49	112	44
Guam	—	—	233	218	50
Hawaii	102	36	112	67	20
Idaho	89	39	30	88	56
Illinois	163	195	144	94	83
Indiana	85	175	92	96	24
Iowa	127	145	84	95	80
Kansas	165	152	127	97	61
Kentucky	225	630	63	102	40
Louisiana	—	11	66	127	45
Maine	118	294	125	167	66
Maryland	56	67	52	69	48
Massachusetts	119	159	77	94	40
Michigan	116	138	142	103	70
Minnesota	112	44	156	98	50
Mississippi	23	303	50	194	37
Missouri	202	154	123	90	30
Montana	130	284	90	79	72
Nebraska	117	226	117	94	59
Nevada	316	979	152	124	54
New Hampshire	97	316	141	101	71
New Jersey	83	46	65	108	40
New Mexico	89	188	71	75	48
New York	96	100	90	95	60
North Carolina	83	59	70	105	40
North Dakota	332	139	154	109	65
Ohio	60	102	64	105	51
Oklahoma	123	198	20	81	59
Oregon	126	144	75	78	63
Pennsylvania	88	80	61	98	63
Puerto Rico	162	342	94	98	23

Table 2-1 (continued)

State or Possession	Fiscal Year				
	1963	1964	1965	1966	1967[a]
Rhode Island	126	112	78	107	57
South Carolina	39	531	73	100	50
South Dakota	145	102	113	97	69
Tennessee	97	229	116	114	78
Texas	68	88	36	103	61
Utah	112	89	127	105	34
Vermont	299	453	184	111	58
Virginia	109	172	50	93	49
Virgin Islands	—	455	146	125	73
Washington	82	64	89	89	24
West Virginia	72	406	61	99	56
Wisconsin	95	50	69	90	64
Wyoming	194	116	87	117	69
Total	99	141[b]	87[c]	99	55

[a] Percent computation is based on fiscal year 1967 commitments as of December 31, 1966.

[b] Fiscal year 1964 program commitments as a proportion of fiscal 1964 appropriations. Allowance payments made subsequent to June 30, 1964, were charged to fiscal year 1965 appropriation. MDTA amendments of April, 1965 permitted total allowance costs to be committed at time of project approval.

[c] Fiscal year 1965 program commitments as a proportion of fiscal 1965 appropriations. Balance of fiscal year 1965 appropriation required to finance allowance costs for fiscal year 1964 program paid July 1, 1964, or thereafter.

SOURCE: all data throughout this and following tables are from the U.S. Department of Labor unless otherwise specified.

questered in a national pool to assure complete utilization. However, the supplemental amount was not appropriated until June, 1964, and then it totaled only $20 million (see Table 2–2). Only twenty-eight states had used their full apportionment but a large backlog of projects existed, and $68 million of the fiscal 1965 appropriation was required to pay allowances to trainees enrolled in fiscal 1964.

Again in fiscal 1965, by the time the appropriation was approved in September, 60 percent of it was obligated. The appropriation was again $103 million short, and by December 31st only 10 percent remained unobligated. This remaining sum was put into a national pool while a supplemental appropriation was pending. The supplement came in May but amounted to only $89 million. In spite of the scramble to

Table 2–2
MDTA Authorizations and Appropriations

Fiscal Year	1963	1964	1965	1966	1967	1968
			(in thousands of dollars)			
Legislative Authorization	100,000	165,000	411,000	454,000	a	a
Original Appropriation	70,147	110,000	307,906	434,991	421,041	385,490
Supplemental Amount		20,000	89,000			
Total Obligated	70,026	129,310	394,640	434,515	420,366	—

a The 1966 amendments deleted reference to an authorization ceiling.

obligate these late funds, over $2 million remained uncommitted and was reclaimed by the Treasury.

Those states which got more than "their share" considered the process equitable, but others, including New York, which was consistently slow in committing its allocation, complained. The vocational educators, accustomed to an unconditional grant-in-aid system, most resented the reallocation procedure. The uncertainty as to whether and when reallocation might occur made planning difficult for all and encouraged a scramble to commit funds early in the fiscal year. At the behest of Senator Javits, backed by Representative Goodell, reapportionment was limited to the last half of the year with thirty days' notice required during the third quarter. After March 31st, funds not used could be placed in a national pool without notice. The mortgage on each new appropriation to pay training allowances for previously funded projects was eliminated by authorizing use of the approval year's funds for allowances as well as training costs during the succeeding year.

Incorporation of ARA Training

Beginning in 1962, the training provisions of the Area Redevelopment Act had been administered concurrently with MDTA but under separate authority. In 1965, the demise of ARA and its replacement by the Economic Development Administration was imminent. The ARA training provisions had more restrictive training allowances than MDTA but were more generous, since all the unemployed and underemployed in a redevelopment area were eligible, no state matching was required, and there were no state apportionments. The amended Act simply adopted the most generous provisions of both programs as Section 241 of MDTA.

Other Areas of Concern

Despite evidence of general congressional confidence in the administrators of the program, the Senate took the occasion to request more and better evaluations of program results. The House went further, complaining, as both houses had done in 1963, that on-the-job training was still inadequately used, though they warned against substitution of federal support for existing private efforts. The congressmen also expressed concern that too many participants were being trained for low-wage occupations and that the Labor Department had not been sufficiently aggressive in establishing effective local advisory committees. The House complaints also reflected the concern of some labor unions that the extension of the training period to 104 weeks might lead to interference in apprenticeable trades.

Nearly all issues were worked out satisfactorily in committee, leaving the amendments with clear sailing on the floor of both houses. Senators Prouty and Murphy failed in their bid to limit the extension of the Act until June 30, 1967, and even they assured the Senate that they wished only to allow continuous review, not to threaten MDTA's life. Once again, support was overwhelming. The Senate voted 76–9 for the amendments, and the House endorsed them unanimously. The program had progressed to a state of ostensible permanence, with, as an accomplished fact, full federal financing and the first implications of objectives that went beyond facilitating the employment of the unemployed.

THE 1966 AMENDMENTS

By 1966 Congressional support was so overwhelming that a House bill amending the Act was passed by voice vote under suspension of the rules. The Senate subcommittee heard only one witness, Assistant Secretary of Labor for Manpower Stanley Ruttenberg, and asked him only one question, "Would you agree that there is nothing controversial in these amendments which would cause any particular delay in the Committee meeting and marking up the bill and reporting it to the floor?" The Senate bill, identical to that of the House, was reported and passed unanimously even before the floor manager, Senator Clark, could arrive to speak on its behalf.

It was not that the amendments were without substance. Significant changes were made, but they were continuations of the trends of earlier amendments and seemed to be totally without opposition. The amendments were also in harmony with the current issues and trends in congressional thinking. Perhaps equally responsible for the favorable reaction was the fact that neither the 1965 nor the 1966 amendments required additional funds but only involved greater permissiveness in the use of existing budgets.

By the summer of 1966, the unemployment rate was hovering around 3.8 percent. Only fourteen areas had substantial or persistent unemployment, as compared with forty-eight in the same period in 1962. Despite complaints of local stringencies from employers, there were no general shortages of manpower. There were still heavy concentrations of unemployment in inner-city ghettos and depressed rural areas, but the problems were clearly not on the scale of those of 1962 or even of early 1965. A decision had been made during the spring of 1966 to concentrate efforts for fiscal 1967 on two problems: "the emergence of selected skill shortages that accompany declining unemployment and the residual pockets of hard-core unemployment levels."[15] The former was to absorb 35 percent of Title II funds and the latter 65 percent.

[15] U.S., Congress, House, Committee on Education and Labor, Select Subcommittee on Labor, *Manpower Development and Training Act Amendments of 1966, Hearings on H.R. 14690*, 89th Cong., 2d sess., 1966, p. 61.

The Proposals

A number of bills had been introduced in the House to facilitate the proposed reorientation and to broaden administrative discretion. One proposal redefined basic education to include communications skills and work habits. Another sought to provide physical examinations and minor health services, hoping to cut rejections, absences, and dropouts for health reasons. Despite the fact that workers over forty-five years of age made up more than a quarter of the unemployed, they represented only 10 percent of MDT trainees. Though nothing in the existing Act prevented it, specific direction was sought in one proposal for a special training program for older workers. Another proposal directed the Secretary of Labor to institute training programs in penal institutions to prepare inmates for successful employment upon release, despite prohibition of such training by an internal Labor Department directive in 1963. Subsidization of wages to encourage on-the-job training and a weekly allowance of $20 plus a reasonable expense allowance for MDT trainees on welfare was also proposed.

Several bills were designed to loosen eligibility requirements. They sought to reduce the labor force attachment required for training allowances from two years to one, pay allowances to youths who had been out of school less than one year if they had dependents, and offer a second chance if a training program failed to provide a job. An emergency loan fund for trainees was also proposed. The most significant proposal, by Congressmen Holland and O'Hara, sought to eliminate the "reasonable expectations of employment" requirement for disadvantaged workers and allow training whenever it would increase their employability.

Two amendments advocated increased administrative discretion. One suggested an unallocated reserve of 20 percent of the Title II funds, to be used at the discretion of the Secretary of Labor and the Secretary of Health, Education, and Welfare without application of the state apportionment formula. The other proposed broader authority to provide training directly through public or private institutions where a state was unwilling to do so.

The Amendments

Only proposals for subsidizing wage costs ran into any substantial opposition. Secretary of Labor Wirtz was opposed to the idea, though he admitted that some of the training cost reimbursements already being paid in MDT-OJT projects were little more than subsidies.[16] AFL-CIO witnesses also expressed opposition.[17] They were also concerned that training in penal institutions not violate their historical opposition to prison labor and were disturbed that training for "increased employability" rather than "reasonable expectations of employment" might create surplus skills. They questioned allowances for part-time training of employed persons and wanted it clear that public education facilities should have priority over private ones, but on none of these points were they adamant.

The wage subsidy proposal disappeared in the House subcommittee. Authority to make advances on training allowances was substituted for the loan fund. The requirement that a youth be out of school at least one year before MDT enrollment could be waived by certification that return to school was unlikely and impractical. The Secretary of Labor was relieved of responsibility for a training report separate from the *Manpower Report*, though the HEW report was continued. The Secretary of HEW was directed to "give preference to training from state education agencies" but was authorized to bypass them and contract directly with public or private institutions whenever "it would permit persons to begin their training edu-

[16] *Ibid.*, pp. 57, 85.
[17] *Ibid.*, p. 100.

cation within a shorter period of time, or permit the needed training or education to be provided more economically, or more effectively."

The "reasonable expectation of employment" prerequisite was retained for skill training, but "improving employability" was substituted as adequate justification for basic education and the newly authorized "communication skills." All other proposals emerged unchanged. In addition, the relocation and bonding experiments were extended. Neighborhood Youth Corps graduates were made eligible for MDT courses without a waiting period and with full rather than youth allowances in order to prevent the drop from the higher NYC stipend from discouraging them from MDT training. The Appropriations Committee later refused to fund the health services and prison training provisions, but these decisions were probably attributable more to lobbying from competing federal agencies than to congressional reluctance.

EVOLUTION OF MDTA

By the end of 1967, MDTA was quite a different program in legislative direction, in administrative practice, and even in declared objectives, than it had been in 1962. A bill extending MDTA was introduced by Senators Clark and Prouty at the close of 1967, though no changes in the legislation were proposed by the Administration or Congress. However, there is no reason to believe that the legislative evolution has ended, nor that it will not continue to be characterized by flexibility and bipartisanship.

Most of the legislative changes occurring in 1963, 1965, and 1966 were in harmony with the preferences of one or another of the early advocates of a federally sponsored remedial training program, but it is doubtful whether any of them could have foreseen the current Act or designed it as it is. With one exception—refresher courses for professional employees—no significant change has been made in the original statement of findings and purpose, but substantively the Act is more in harmony with that rhetoric than it was in 1962.

In effect, an emergency recession measure designed to provide technologically displaced, experienced, family heads with subsistence while they acquired new skills through either state-operated vocational schools or private on-the-job training in order to fill existing job vacancies has become a permanent, wide-ranging, primarily federally financed and directed program, though with less clearly defined objectives than the original bill. Currently, the emphasis is on assisting those with a wide variety of disadvantages to become effective competitors in the labor market. However, the professional refresher and part-time upgrading components and the rhetoric of alleviating labor shortages indicate a trend toward a general-purpose, remedial, out-of-school training program.

The time span of the original bill was four years, with considerable support for limiting it to two. For all intents and purposes, the program is now permanent, with expiration dates providing no more than a convenient opportunity for congressional review. The Act was originally designed for family heads of substantial skill and long-term labor force attachment. However, there was never any limitation on who could be trained as long as the trainees could be defined as unemployed or underemployed. The restrictions on eligibility applied only to training allowances. In 1961 and 1962, a reluctant Congress would not authorize more than 5 percent of training allowance expenditures to aid out-of-school youths. Eligibility for basic adult allowances has since been broadened to include any unemployed person with one year's employment experience if he is either a head of a household or a member of a household with an unemployed head, plus former NYC enrollees. In addition, youths seventeen to twenty-one years of age are eligible for a $20 allowance as long as local education authorities conclude that school attendance is "no longer practicable." Even the employed are eligible for a $10 weekly incentive for part-time training, while public assistance recipients are encouraged to become employable by an additional $20 a week incentive payment plus reimbursement for out-of-pocket expenses.

Training allowances for adults in 1961 were limited to the average unemployment compensation payment in the state of residence. With the addition of $10 to the basic allowance plus up to $20 in dependency allowances, the average adult weekly maximum allowance has risen from $35 in 1963 to $54 in 1967, which includes commuting costs but not the travel and subsistence payments available to those who must be away from home for training. The eligibility period has increased from 52 to 104 weeks. The course content has progressed from skill training to basic education, prevocational training, preapprenticeship training, professional refresher courses, grooming, communications skills, or any other type of training which would increase not only "reasonable expectation of employment" but also access to skill training.

Congress has moved away from its original preference for state matching toward the Labor Department's original proposal for permanent federal funding, though the 10 percent "in kind" matching requirement is retained to give an aura of state responsibility (about one-third of the total state share is paid in cash). The jockeying between federal and state control of allocation has resulted in a compromise, with the apportionment formula inviolate during the first six months of each fiscal year but with 20 percent of Title II funds reserved for federal discretion and with state review and approval of small contracts within tight federal guidelines. Programs not initially acceptable to Congress—training in correctional institutions, relocation, and bonding—have been tolerated as long as they were noted as "experimental and demonstration projects" but so far have been refused Title II funds.

Congress has, in general, given whatever authority was requested, but its support has never been put to the real test. Requests for broadened authority have not been accompanied by corresponding requests for funding. The result has been authorization for enrichment of services but only at the price of reduction in the numbers served, leaving administrators with a difficult choice between a richer program for fewer or a leaner program for more.

3:

Organizing To Deliver Service

LEGISLATION and appropriation are only necessary first steps in the delivery of program services. MDTA had both the advantage and the disadvantage, as compared with the anti-poverty program launched two years later, of having available established federal and state agencies to begin immediate training activity. Some projects were approved and some trainees enrolled within the very month in which funds were appropriated. The job to be done—identification of unemployed workers needing training, pinpointing of occupations promising reasonable expectations of employment, and establishment of training projects to bring the two together—had few unfamiliar aspects, although the clientele was somewhat unfamiliar. On the other hand, the shortcomings, the prejudices, and the conflicts of the agencies involved were built into the new program.

The Act placed joint responsibility upon the Secretary of Labor and the Secretary of Health, Education, and Welfare but gave clear primacy to the former. Most important, MDTA appropriations were made to the Labor Department with HEW commitments honored from that source. With dollars went power. In addition, the Act gave to the Secretary of Labor responsibility for research, experimentation, and demonstration, the preparation of the *Manpower Report of the President*, the identification of employment opportunities and eligible trainees, the payment of allowances, supervision of on-the-job training, and placement of those who completed training. The Secretary of Health, Education, and Welfare was authorized only to contract for training in educational institutions. This division of authority, resulting as it did from the combining of an Administration bill giving full authority to the Secretary of Labor with the original Senate bill favoring HEW, reflects not only the persuasiveness of the former but also the initial disinterest of the latter. There were too many claimants for the new responsibilities in the Department of Labor and too few in Health, Education, and Welfare.

ADMINISTRATIVE STRUCTURE IN
THE LABOR DEPARTMENT

INTERNAL COMPETITION

The Department of Labor in 1962 was a conglomeration of autonomous enclaves, some with independent power bases, linked by interests in labor market institutions and problems that were widely divergent. Its most recent, present, and future secretaries had been or would be chosen from among experts in labor-management relations. The internal competitors for MDT responsibility were the United States Employment Service (USES), the Bureau of Apprenticeship and Training (BAT), and the Office of Manpower, Automation, and Training (OMAT). The first was a unit, along with the Unemployment Insurance Service, of the Bureau of Employment Security (BES), placing it at the third tier of departmental authority, visibility, and prestige. Its funding source was Title III of the Social Security Act, which allocated a portion of the unemployment insurance payroll tax revenues for the maintenance of the USES to provide a work test for eligibility of unemployment insurance recipients. Therefore, its budget, along with that of the rest of BES, was, to a considerable extent, independent of the Department. It also had an independent power base in the Interstate Conference of Employment Security Agencies, which held veto power over policies through influence with the appropriations committees in

Congress. USES in turn provided 100 percent of the budgets of the affiliated state employment services. It had authority to establish standards for the operations of the nearly 2,000 state employment service offices but had little political power to exercise that authority.

The USES was in the throes of reorganization. After an impressive performance in coordinating World War II and Korean War manpower policy, the Service lost momentum during the 1950's. In 1958 Secretary of Labor James P. Mitchell had castigated the agency for a declining placement rate and unsatisfactory employer relations. The organizational implications of his criticisms were the consolidation of small employment service offices into larger, more attractive ones in downtown areas where employers were located, specialization by occupational grouping, placement of emphasis on services for the growing white-collar and professional occupations, and establishment of placements as the measure of success. How ever, the necessary funds did not become available until fiscal 1962. Thus, redirection began on the eve of policy decisions which, though it was not immediately apparent, would have inconsistent implications.

The BES was less than enthusiastic about MDTA, in part because of its doubts about the relationship between training allowances and unemployment compensation. On the other hand, the USES was anxious to have primary responsibility for the new program.

The Bureau of Apprenticeship and Training had as its responsibility the promotion and registering of labor–management-sponsored apprenticeships. The choice of apprentices, training methods, and costs of training were totally matters decided by local unions and employers. Its power bases were the Building Trades, Metal Trades, and Printing Trades, departments of the AFL-CIO, with a potent assist from the fact that the chairman of the Labor Department-HEW Appropriations Subcommittee was a former Building Trades man. The

BAT administrator was selected after consultation with the craft unions, and most of the field staff were former union officials or journeymen. In most states, BAT had no state counterpart equivalent to the state employment services. Many within the Department of Labor doubted BAT's ability to handle the on-the-job training (OJT) portion of MDT, and many within the Bureau itself were no more anxious to undertake the task. The AFL-CIO was interested in limiting state discretion in the program, particularly in having OJT contracts reviewed and approved at the national level to minimize interference with apprenticeable occupations. BAT was given the OJT assignments, but initially it was given no commensurate expansion of staff to carry out the responsibility.

The third competitor for MDT responsibility was a new agency with no external affiliates but with close relations to and internal support from the Secretary of Labor. An Office of Manpower and Automation had been established as one of the first acts of Secretary of Labor Arthur Goldberg, former General Counsel for the United Steelworkers of America, reflecting the concern within the labor movement and the country in general for the employment impact of new technologies. With the passage of MDTA, the word "training" was added to the new agency's title, and OMAT became for a time the dominant agency in departmental decisions related to the new program.

The situation was an unstable one. OMAT had the Secretary's support, but his major involvement was in resolving labor disputes, and he made no firm decisions in the internal conflict over MDTA authority. The USES, while lacking an internal top-level champion, had the only organizational capacity at the local level. As a local arm of the program, the state employment services were responsible, under their contract with the Labor Department, for identifying, screening, and referring trainees, determining appropriate training occupations, and placing enrollees after training. The state vocational education agencies, with ties to the HEW Office of

Education as the other local arm, contracted to provide the training. Initially, proposed institutional training projects were reviewed and approved by tripartite federal teams representing OMAT, BES, and HEW, but the final authority was held by the director of OMAT. On-the-job training was undertaken by employers under direct contracts with BAT.

OMAT developed a potent weapon in its administration of the entire MDTA appropriation, including the HEW portion. The local sponsors were accused of "creaming" the unemployed, and budgetary authority was used to fund "experimental and demonstration" projects aimed at the more disadvantaged. The old-line agencies, already smarting from OMAT's brashness, including its recruiting of their personnel, considered this an unjustified allocation of funds. Since OMAT's weakness was lack of state and local affiliates, the new agency began installing representatives in major cities to deal directly with and coordinate the efforts of the state and local agencies. Field offices were set up in fourteen cities before departmental competitors caught on and used their influence to halt the development. With neither a political constituency nor a local administrative arm, OMAT's dominance was inevitably shortlived. Arguments continue as to whether its initial dominance got the new program off the ground faster than might otherwise have been the case.

THE MANPOWER ADMINISTRATION

In February, 1963, Secretary of Labor W. Willard Wirtz attempted to calm the internecine warfare within his department by appointing his Undersecretary, John L. Henning, as Manpower Administrator to exercise control over the quarreling principalities. An Office of Financial and Management Services was established, reporting directly to the Manpower Administrator, to coordinate the budgetary activities of the three bureaus. However, each bureau retained its own budget office and appropriation, its administrative staff, its separate operations and organizational identity, and its independent field structure. The Undersecretary was left with a mediator's role, which turned out to be more than a part-time one.

During succeeding months the Vocational Education Act of 1963 requiring USES involvement, the Senate passage of the Youth Employment Act, and the beginning discussions of an antipoverty program, added to the MDTA experience, made it apparent that the Department's expansion would be in manpower programs rather than in labor-management relations and labor market statistics. In April, 1964, a full-time Manpower Administrator, John C. Donovan, was named; he exercised greater control than his predecessor, though he lacked a central staff directly responsible to him.

With the passage of the Economic Opportunity Act, another manpower agency, the Neighborhood Youth Corps (NYC), later called the Bureau of Work and Training Programs (BWTP), was added to the Manpower Administration to administer the program delegated from the Office of Economic Opportunity. The BES-OMAT conflict was resolved first by giving the BES authority for approval of institutional training projects and limiting OMAT to planning, research, demonstration, and evaluation; later changing its name to the Office of Manpower Policy, Evaluation, and Research (OMPER); and finally eliminating it as a separate office within the Manpower Administration. A management consultant firm was also hired to study further administrative reforms.

Donovan resigned in February, 1965, and Stanley H. Ruttenberg, formerly director of research for the AFL-CIO and a special assistant to Secretary Wirtz, became Manpower Administrator and subsequently Assistant Secretary for Manpower. Ruttenberg began to exercise more forceful control but had no sooner taken office than the previously employed management consulting firm returned its report recommending dissolution of BES, including its regional offices, the financial functions within BAT, the BAT regional offices, and the OMAT field offices. Directors of BAT, USES, the Unemployment Insurance Service, and NYC would report directly to the Manpower and Employment Security Administration, as would regional manpower and employment security administrators. As soon as the report was circulated within the Department, it came to the attention of the Interstate Conference of Employment Security Agencies, the AFL-CIO Building Trades Department, and the House Appropriations Subcommittee chairman. The reaction of the last was decisive: attempts to implement the recommendations would mean no budget for the Manpower Administration.

The elimination of the OMAT field staff was the only immediate result, but time appears to be on the side of the Manpower Administration. With a change of House Appropriations Subcommittee chairmen, regional manpower administrators were approved in the fiscal 1968 budget, though BES and BAT regional administrators continue under each regional manpower administrator. In December, 1967, OJT authority was removed from BAT and given to the Bureau of Work and Training programs. BES through USES retained institutional training responsibilities, though it was apparent that even those had been in doubt for a time. The Manpower Administration was apparently centralizing the manpower and antipoverty program responsibilities, leaving the old-line bureaus with their traditional responsibilities but contracting for the newer services directly with state and local agencies or private institutions.

ADMINISTRATIVE STRUCTURE OF HEW

By contrast, HEW showed little initial interest in the new Act. The vocational education emphasis of the original Clark bill was there because of state, not national, interest. It was primarily the efforts of the American Vocational Association that offset the preferences of the Bureau of the Budget and the Labor Department for a program with the latter as sole federal sponsor. The criticisms by President Kennedy's Panel on Vocational Education were a source of further reluctance to involve the Office of Education (OE). HEW was not significantly involved in designing the Act, and after its passage neither the Secretary nor the Commissioner of Education appeared enthusiastic about their new responsibility.

The resulting uncertainty in the establishment of administrative procedures within HEW prevented the latter from assuming a full partnership role in the formative period. Responsibility was first lodged in the Office of the Undersecretary, who delegated direct state contacts to OE's Division of Vocational Education, thus in fact bypassing the Commissioner of Education. This much-criticized division was undergoing a personnel squeeze, and the 160 slots available for MDT were a bonanza. Two small branches were created, a Program Operations Branch for project review and approval and a Program Services Branch for teacher training and development of training materials. All other functions were assigned to regular offices within the Division. Soon, with two HEW reorganizations in anticipation of and consequent to the passage of the Vocational Education Act of 1963, people paid with MDT funds were scattered throughout HEW.

The Labor Department's control of the budget meant it would be at least senior partner in administering the Act. HEW's response assured that initial MDT policy decisions would be Labor's by default. In 1966 MDT activities were finally consolidated and elevated to the status of a separate division parallel to and on an equal level with the Division of Vocational and Technical Education. MDT authority was transferred from the Office of the Undersecretary to the Commissioner of Education, who could rule in his own office. The new Division of Manpower Development and Training then began a struggle for a stronger voice in MDTA policy, but it remained handicapped by history.

ADMINISTRATIVE CONFLICTS

The new program was launched with the handicaps of divided authority, complex administrative procedures, and limited experience. However, intra-agency conflicts were more troublesome than inter-agency ones.

The state employment services were jealous of their independence, but they had been federalized during World War II. More important, their funding was fully federal and was allocated among the states by formulas which were developed by the USES rather than determined legislatively. The state services complained that they were being burdened with new tasks without an adequate increase in resources, to the detriment of their existing functions. They were accustomed to working through their states and the regional offices of the USES as their route to Washington, and they considered the OMAT field representatives to be interlopers. They were conditioned to providing the best available applicants to fill employer job orders and thus were likely to "cream" those eligible for MDT. The concept of "outreach" to search out and bring in the disadvantaged awaited development by the Economic Opportunity Act's Community Action Agencies after 1964. Nevertheless, most of the state and local employment services accepted their new MDT responsibilities and pursued them with a reasonable degree of vigor.

BAT field staff were both few in number and unenthusiastic about the MDT assignment. Their craft union loyalties often made them suspicious of the new program's impact on the apprenticeable trades. Therefore, on-the-job training remained an underdeveloped aspect of the program until high-level pressures were exerted in 1965.

State and local vocational educators were accustomed to federal grants-in-aid with no strings attached other than the requirement that they be used within broad occupational groupings. The latter were fixed by legislation going back to 1917 and tended to restrict adjustment of vocational education programs to changes in the occupational structure. Even under the G.I. Bill, state vocational educators had been granted large sums of federal money and allowed to use it with little or no federal surveillance. They resented the project-by-project federal review and approval process and the accompanying paperwork. They, like the state employment services, were unaccustomed to serving the disadvantaged. Through the American Vocational Association, they bombarded Congress with their complaints, stories of excessive delays in project approval, and pictures of two-foot-high stacks of forms required for a single project, failing to note that state as well as federal requirements added to the height of the stack.[1]

Delays were a serious problem, with two to six months elapsing from the conception of a project to enrollment and training of the unemployed. Approving and funding projects involved two lines of administrative authority at four levels. Local employment service personnel, acting for their state agency, identified eligible potential trainees and made labor market surveys to ascertain a reasonable expectation of employment following training. This information, once it reached the state level, was given to state vocational education officials so that they could designate a school for the training. Back at the local level again, school officials had to find buildings, space, equipment, tools, supplies, and instructors and supervisors not already absorbed by regular school activities.

Employment service and vocational education personnel then had to specify trainee selection standards and referral procedures, obtain curriculum materials, select teachers and

[1] *Nation's Manpower Revolution*, pt. 6:2051–2123.

counselors, and plan reporting and placement procedures. Budgets had to be prepared to cover the employment service testing, counseling, screening and selection, training allowance and placement costs, and the school's costs for salaries, equipment, supplies, in-school counseling, and reporting and evaluation. The completed project proposal then required state review and finally a meeting with a federal review team from the regional offices of the two agencies. Initially, many projects were passed on to the national agencies for final approval, and unusual, large, or multioccupational projects continued to stream into Washington for some time. The on-the-job training project approval was less complex but not necessarily faster. Both potential trainees and potential jobs sometimes disappeared in the process.

Gradually, procedures were simplified and authority decentralized. Basically, however, the administrative structure never changed. Delays are no longer a general problem, primarily because those involved have learned to live with the system and because subsequent projects have tended to settle into a routine of training for the same occupations with committed facilities and personnel.

National objectives often clashed with local customs and mores. Both the BES and vocational education at the national level reflected the local orientation of their constituent state agencies. However, the USES director and the MDT staff were more committed to national objectives, which began to favor the competitively disadvantaged. Neither local employment services nor schools were accustomed to serving those with the most serious employment handicaps, and they resisted the change.

Service to minority groups was a particular problem. Neither the Labor Department nor HEW was anxious to confront the issue in the South for fear that states would simply withdraw from the program. In fact, Louisiana initially refused to participate, and the director of vocational education from another southern state contacted his counterparts throughout the nation advocating refusal of MDT funds. State affiliates of both agencies customarily functioned on a segregated basis in the South. The USES, with its full federal financing and a tradition of mild federal guidelines, found it easier to root out discrimination. Vocational education in the South was primarily white. A struggle was required to get Negroes into the program and then to end segregated instruction once both races were admitted. Training for blue-collar jobs was finally integrated to a reasonable degree, but eventually a nationwide contract with an association of private business schools was needed to establish desegregated classes in white-collar occupations.

Vocational educators were accustomed to training high school youths six hours a day for two years and to holding part-time evening classes for employed adults. MDT involved dealing with unemployed workers seeking jobs and anxious to minimize training time. The tempo was intensive—forty hours a week with frequent round-the-clock operations.

Accustomed to unfettered grants-in-aid, the vocational educators tended to look at the 100 percent federal MDT support in the same proprietary sense and resented administrative direction. The issues were confronted one by one, and after five years most state and local personnel in both the employment services and the vocational education hierarchies are committed to the program and tolerate federal direction; however, they still consider themselves more aware of local needs than "the feds." The willingness of vocational educators to work within federal guidelines with MDT funds does not reflect any change in attitude in the use of federally matched vocational funds.

With the passage of time, inter-agency conflicts in the MDTA administration appear least serious at the local level and strongest at the national level, but at neither level are they serious enough to impede the program. Most conflicts have involved inter-bureau differences in orientation rather than inter-agency disputes, though the former often cross agency lines. Initially, BES and the Division of Vocational Education were aligned against OMAT on the issue of experimental and demonstration projects, a position that largely reflected the clash of a local versus national orientation. The unfortunate result was a reduced learning value from the E & D projects, which tended to be isolated from regular MDT operations. As more emphasis was placed on OJT, BAT became a competitor for budgets against the Office of Education's Division of Manpower Development and Training and the USES, which by now had a strong commitment to institutional training. Yet until OJT authority was removed from BAT, they and the OE tended to ally themselves against the Manpower Administrator, both resenting the latter's increasing exercise of overall program control.

Initially, the weakness of the HEW structure reduced the incidence of policy conflicts. Resentment over Labor Department budgetary control and feelings that the Vocational Education Division was receiving less than its share of the personnel allocation never came to the surface as a serious issue. At one point, officials of the Division of Vocational Education complained that they learned of new projects from the newspapers. The Labor Department countered that HEW staff, when informed in advance of projects being reviewed, often informed congressmen, who thereupon made premature announcements in their districts. This practice tied the hands of review teams, who then could no longer turn down ill-conceived projects.

Within the OE's Division of Manpower Development and Training, mild resentment at Labor Department dominance turned to a restive attempt to assert a policy-making voice. There were complaints that the 20 percent of Title II funds authorized as an unallocated reserve to be used at the discretion of the two secretaries, unrestrained by the state allocation formula, were being used unilaterally by the Manpower Administrator. A unilateral Labor Department decision to raise the 1967 OJT component to one-half the total number of training "slots" was criticized for creating idle institutional capacity. The sole Labor Department authority over Title I experimental and demonstration funds is another source of frustration. So far the resentment has not flared into personal acrimony. The outbreak of a power struggle is possible, but the Labor Department appears to have the more formidable artillery.

NEW ADMINISTRATIVE MECHANISMS

The passage of MDTA found vocational education facilities already inadequate to meet their regular enrollments, yet the Act contemplated no building of new facilities. No machinery existed for public encouragement of on-the-job training. The legislation placed new strains on federal-state-local relationships and required new methods of inter-agency coordination. The advent of overlapping antipoverty legislation added to the administrative complexities. Each of these issues had to be confronted and solutions developed.

MULTIOCCUPATIONAL PROJECTS
AND SKILL CENTERS

Initially, most MDT projects were conducted during off hours in public school facilities. These facilities were soon fully utilized, and it became necessary to rent space and secure equipment, some from government surplus sources. MDT money could be used for modifications of buildings as well as for purchase of equipment, but not for new construction. Little use was made of private schools, primarily because of the role of the state boards of education in designating training locations at the local level. The federal agencies used their private contracting authority only as a detour around recalcitrant local school boards. The number of MDT enrollees in private schools has increased, but it still amounts to only 5 percent of total enrollments (Table 3–1). The trend in institutional training has been toward totally MDT-supported skill centers. However, the trend is the product of pedagogical problems, philosophical issues, and changing program objectives, as well as the shortage of facilities.

MDT was initially conceived simply as vocational education with subsistence allowances for adult workers. Many new problems emerged almost immediately and required *ad hoc* answers. The small ($10 million) ARA retraining program established a pattern which affected the conduct of the more general manpower training program. Since ARA's primary purpose was to train workers to meet the specific needs of a particular employer, and thus to attract new industry to the location, the logical approach was a separate training project for each occasion. Since MDTA had as its goal any employment with any employer, eligible persons could simply have been integrated into existing vocational courses, but the pat-

Table 3–1

Number of Trainees Approved for Institutional Training, by Type of Training Facility and Project

Training Facility and Project	Fiscal Year			
	1963	1964	1965	1966
Public	*55,307*	*108,653*	*159,067*	*141,342*
Single occupation	55,307	68,246	108,576	105,428
Multiple occupation	—	40,407	49,223	32,072
Individual referral	—	—	1,268	3,842
Private	*1,556*	*4,918*	*9,391*	*8,157*
Single occupation	1,556	3,693	7,036	7,002
Multiple occupation	—	1,225	2,295	1,155
Individual referral	—	—	60	—
Not Reported	*223*	*890*	*460*	*895*
Total	57,086	114,461	168,918	150,394

tern had been set. In addition, in the few places where appropriate vocational classes were available, they were usually full to capacity. Enrollment was limited to a September starting date, and training methods were controlled by the more leisurely patterns of full-time students. There was also reluctance to include with the regular student body unemployed adults who were being paid to attend. Individual enrollments were nil at first, though they have grown slowly since.

The separate-project approach, on the other hand, presented a philosophical dilemma. The potential trainee was being denied a meaningful occupational choice: either he accepted the training course being established or he remained unemployed. Employment service personnel attempted to alleviate the problem by filling out "interest cards" advising applicants of future training possibilities. But the future offering was usually limited also, and the need was for immediate employment. In one internal Labor Department study 35 percent of the trainees questioned reported that they would have preferred training for a different occupation, had it been available.

As the emphasis on youth and the disadvantaged became greater, concern over this limited occupational choice increased. The potential trainees lacked work experience and exposure to alternative occupational possibilities. Their educational backgrounds were often too limited to qualify them for training in the more promising occupations. Through trial and error, the answer was found in the multioccupational project and the skill center. Starting in 1964, proposals were developed for training in a single project several hundred students in as many as fifteen to twenty different occupations. Trainees, mostly youths, entered a prevocational orientation phase of counseling, basic education, and brief exposure to a number of occupational offerings. They then settled on an occupation, continuing basic education as needed.

School facilities were not generally available for the multi-occupational projects, and it was frequently necessary to install equipment in an idle factory or similar site. These projects often appeared to be the most successful because of the attitudes of school dropouts and undereducated adults toward their earlier school experience. The evolution toward separate MDT skill centers was natural.

The skill center concept was initiated by OE officials whose responsibility it was to contract for facilities. While the Detroit Skill Center was not the first, its development is typical. MDT classes got off to an early start in September, 1962 using the facilities of a post-secondary vocational school on a 4 P.M. to midnight shift. The Detroit schools were unable to provide facilities for expansion of the program. Vacant garages were rented for auto repair courses; employers were persuaded to rent their establishments at night; equipment was purchased and scattered throughout various high schools.

One of the most successful courses was a practical nursing program. Demand seemed almost unlimited, but adequate space for the course was not available. Coincidentally, the Detroit schools were purchasing land adjacent to a hospital. Since there was a vacant building on the land, the situation was ideal for a Practical Nurse Training Center just for MDT purposes. By the end of 1963, in addition to the nursing program, there were twenty-two individual projects scattered around the city, and the very active Local Manpower Advisory Committee recommended that they be consolidated in an urban training center.

A surplus federal building was purchased for one dollar and equipped partly with surplus federal property and partly through either loans by businesses or purchases. Many of the programs were consolidated, and others became "satellite programs," supervised by the center staff. Basic education, which included instruction in work attitudes and grooming as well as the Three R's, was added. Counselors assigned by the state employment service provided counseling, testing, and placement.

In Newark, New Jersey, where vocational education was a county responsibility, the schools were not cooperative. Federal officials pressed the state either to take over MDT responsibilities in Newark or to certify they could not provide the training, thus permitting direct federal contracting. The state stepped in, remodeled a former teachers' college, and established the Newark Skill Center under state auspices. In Oakland, California, lack of adequate vocational education facilities led to establishment of the Oakland-East Bay Skill Center.

By the close of 1967, there were 108 training facilities exclusively for MDT throughout the country, with a total training capacity of over 67,000. Between 70 and 80 of these sites met the formal definition of a skill center: a central facility serving all types of trainees and providing counseling, prevocational, training, basic education, and skill training in a wide variety of occupations. Nearly one-third of institutional enrollments were in these facilities.

The skill centers had profound administrative implications as well. MDT was inaugurated on the premise that job vacancies could be identified and unemployed persons trained to fill them. The initial local reaction was to require certainty of employment, even to the point of demanding written promises from prospective employers. This interpretation led the House Appropriations Subcommittee to admonish the administrators that "reasonable expectation does not mean certainty." But the skill center approach implies even greater freedom from commitment to specific job vacancies. Since trainees do not make a vocational choice until a prevocational phase is completed, it is impossible to fix in advance the number to be trained in each occupation. Since the investment for equipment to train persons for a particular occupation is substantial, it is necessary to concentrate on those occupations for which a continuing demand is likely. Yet with the trainee having a choice within the limits of the occupations offered, the needs and wishes of the individual rather than the demands of the labor market become paramount.

Since continuous operation and staffing are implied, project-by-project approval becomes questionable. Large investment implies a substantial continuing commitment which can tie up major portions of a state's allotment. Basic changes in both the philosophy and the administration of the Act are implied. However, just as the skill centers emerged *ad hoc* in answer to similar problems in a wide variety of areas, such changes are likely to come about indirectly.

SUBCONTRACTING ON-THE-JOB TRAINING

The initial expectation of Congress was that approximately one-third of the MDT program would consist of on-the-job training.[2] Instead, the proportion was only 6 percent in 1963, 12 percent in 1964, and 19 percent as late as 1965. Key congressional figures complained periodically that the OJT program had not fulfilled their expectations. The Labor Department initially had distrusted the competence of vocational education to train for successful employment and had preferred the directly relevant approach of OJT. Yet the underutilization of OJT continued, even though the mix of OJT and institutional training was largely a Labor Department decision. A distrust of BAT in other parts of the Department, which appears to have been responsible for restricting its staff, and the early reluctance of BAT personnel to pursue their new assignment vigorously were only part of the explanation. Promoting OJT was simply more difficult than developing institutional projects. As long as potential employment opportu-

---

[2] U.S., Congress, House, Committee on Education and Labor, *Amendments of Manpower Development and Training Act of 1962, Report to Accompany H.R. 8720*, 88th Cong., 1st sess., 1963, H. Rept. 861, p. 14.

nities could be identified and trainees recruited, an institutional training class could be developed. OJT required employer participation, and, in the existing slack labor markets, employers faced few recruiting difficulties.

Industry-sponsored training obviously came cheaper to the public than vocational education: it offered no problems of recruiting instructors, purchasing equipment, keeping up with industrial developments, or placing graduates. But employers were reluctant to offer training, sometimes because they lacked the resources and ability, but more often because training is a risky investment. The skills thus gained belong not to the firm but to the worker, who can leave at will and take his newly acquired skills to a competing employer.

The basic purpose of MDT-OJT was to reduce through public subsidy employers' reluctance to train. However, the program could reimburse employers only for training costs. Allowances could not be used as wage subsidies because of political and union opposition and prevailing wage laws. Relatively few employers found the average of $25 per week which could be justified as reimbursement for supervisory time, wastage, and other training costs to be a sufficient incentive when compared with the red tape involved in government programs and with their ability to attract reasonably skilled people in a loose labor market.

As labor markets began to tighten MDT-OJT became increasingly attractive. However, expansion would have been less rapid had it not been for the device of the national OJT contract. Any slackening or resurgence of manufacturing activity is likely to be first felt in the tool and die industry. Little training had been necessary with the slow growth of the late 1950's and early 1960's. By the end of 1964, however, the industry was in need of manpower. Industry officials serving on the Department of Labor's Federal Committee on Apprenticeship seized the opportunity to offset the reluctance to train typical of its individual small employers.

A contract was signed with the National Tool, Die, and Precision Machining Association under which the latter became the prime contractor for 1,200 MDT-OJT slots, subcontracting them to its member firms. A contract with the National Tire Dealers and Retreaders Association preceded this one by five days. Concerned by complaints about the quality of dealers' service, Chrysler Corporation signed a similar contract for training 1,000 automobile mechanics and auto body repairmen. Hospitals, continually plagued by high turnover because of their low wages, were brought into the program through an affiliate of the American Hospital Association. By June, 1967, national and interstate contracts had been signed with sixty-five associations and firms covering 67,000 on-the-job training slots.

The simultaneous growth of MDT-OJT and rising demand raised troublesome questions of the degree to which the government was merely assuming a load employers would otherwise have borne. By reducing the risks and costs of training, how much more training was being generated? The national contract device, by making training an industry responsibility, reduced employer reluctance, but in industries like construction this industry approach to training was already being achieved through private collective bargaining. MDT-OJT could be justified as a cheaper substitute for the 100 percent public subsidy of institutional projects, but only if the training provided was broader than the employer required so that the social benefits exceeded the private ones.

By 1966, on-the-job enrollments had increased to 29 percent of the MDT enrollments funded, and an administrative goal of 50 percent was established for fiscal 1967. There were several reasons for this decision. Without allowances and using the facilities of employers, OJT costs per trainee were only one-fourth of institutional costs. Costs were rising but budgets were not, and more trainees could be enrolled with the same appropriation by expanding OJT. Institutional training was,

in effect, a hunting license to search for a job, while enrollment in OJT included employment. Follow-up studies found
nine out of ten of those who completed OJT employed, as
compared with three-fourths of those institutionally trained.

Other motivations for expanding OJT were two-edged.
With the unemployment rate below 4 percent, the available
supply of adult, experienced unemployed workers was at a
minimum. The unemployment rate in 1966 among experienced adults aged twenty-five and over was 2.6 percent;
among married men in that age group it was 1.8 percent, and
among white married men of that age it was 1.6 percent. The
unemployment rate for teenagers was still 12.7 percent, for
nonwhites 7.3 percent, and for nonwhite teenagers 25.4 percent. Fragmentary information suggested that ghetto unemployment rates were triple the national averages, in addition to
high rates of underemployment and nonparticipation in the
labor market. Those workers who were attractive to employers
were being recruited and often trained by them. Even greater
economic pressures would be necessary to employ the remainder, and rising prices were already bringing political
pressure to "cool" the economy.

The decision to expand OJT was accompanied by another
one allocating two-thirds of MDT efforts to training those
facing the greatest disadvantages in competing for jobs. Perhaps subsidized on-the-job training was a way to convince
employers to change their hiring practices. On the other hand,
OJT presented difficulties in reaching the disadvantaged. BAT
staffs were still not generally enthusiastic about MDT; neither
were they, their state counterparts, or their local union com-
patriots among the most aggressive champions of the disadvantaged or minority groups. The national trade association
contractors represented employers who were seeking the best
potential employees. The available financial support was small
and ineffective if the potential employee was particularly unattractive or the employer particularly reluctant. Larger busi-

nesses were likely to use objective hiring requirements and to pursue their own recruitment and training efforts. If not, they were more vulnerable to public scrutiny and pressure and therefore were less likely to be following discriminatory practices. The largely untapped resource for substantial progress in OJT was the small employer, who was both harder to reach and "harder to crack."

Expansion of the BAT staff was restrained not only by the old problems but by a "freeze" on expanding federal employment. For that reason, a new promotion device, the "community contract," was developed. Of the 146,000 OJT slots planned for fiscal 1967, state apprenticeship agencies were assigned 25,000, national trade association contractors were responsible for filling another 30,000, and BAT field staff contracted directly with employers for 65,000 slots. In addition, "community contractors" were recruited to undertake an additional 26,000 OJT slots. Of these, nearly 15,000 were assigned to the Urban League in hopes they would be especially interested and successful in promoting jobs with small employers for Negroes. The remainder went to labor unions, community action agencies, and other interested groups.

The BAT-OJT staff, which grew from 49 to 112 between 1965 and 1966 and to 136 in 1967, had responsibility for supervising all prime contractors and monitoring the subcontracts, many of which were for one or two trainees, in addition to its own expanded promotional activities. In California, for instance, a field staff of six had to monitor about 10,000 OJT slots with national and community prime contractors, while another 14,000 slots were delegated to the state apprenticeship agency. Given such pressures, it is not surprising that some employers received subsidies to train their own or new employees whom they would have trained without the program. Enrollment of most disadvantaged groups was increasing as a proportion of institutional trainees, but OJT enrollments were showing no such improvement.

It was largely this continued failure to enroll a satisfactory proportion of the disadvantaged which led to the transfer of OJT authority from BAT to BWTP in 1967. In addition, the slots had gone unfilled, particularly among the community contractors, who lacked the ready-made employer contacts of the national trade associations. On the other hand, those disadvantaged persons who were enrolled had a high probability of continued employment.

Those with institutional training responsibilities complained that the reallocation in favor of OJT left school facilities, and particularly the MDT-financed skill centers, underutilized. A survey made in October, 1967, found the skill centers and other facilities set up exclusively for MDT operating at about 50 percent of capacity. BAT officials countered that, even with the reallocation, only 15 percent of the total MDT budget would be spent for on-the-job training. The goal to fund 250,-000 training slots in fiscal 1967 would have been impossible to attain without the transfer of substantial numbers of trainees to lower-cost OJT.

The relative advantages of OJT and institutional training continue to be a major issue. The important question of the relative *net* addition to total training and employment as a result of the OJT expansion remains unanswered. Nevertheless, the Labor Department retains its original preference for OJT and appears likely to emphasize that portion of the program even more in the future. Throughout fiscal 1967, coupled programs merging institutional training for basic education and prevocational orientation, followed by on-the-job skill training, were stressed. There was no coordination between vocational educators and OJT administrators, however, nor were employers committed in advance to providing OJT opportunities at the close of the institutional phase.

In the summer of 1967, the Labor Department unilaterally launched a new experimental effort. The Department was motivated by the hope of attaining coupling advantages, as well as by the 1967 emphasis on more direct involvement of private employers. Ten contracts were let, eight with private business firms, one with a local school system, and the tenth with a private nonprofit institution. The contractors were to provide or purchase basic education and prevocational training themselves and then, acting as brokers, place the trainees in OJT situations in their own establishments or with other employers. The hope was that one employer would have more influence with another than would the BAT staff or the national and community contractors. Though it is too early to evaluate these so-called MA-1 projects, preliminary reports suggest that, despite costs in excess of the regular coupled programs, the MA-1 contractors are no less given to "creaming" and no more successful in convincing employers, including their own companies, to undertake MDTA-OJT than their predecessors. Undaunted, the Labor Department announced an MA-2 project, letting bid contracts in five cities for employers to take the trainees on their own payrolls from the beginning of the basic and prevocational phases.

STATE AND LOCAL MANPOWER PLANNING

As in most education and training legislation that is aimed at making a significant impact on labor markets, the authors of MDTA sought to involve representatives of those most likely to be interested and helpful as well as those effected who were wary of such planning. This was the impetus for the organization of the National Manpower Advisory Committee as well as the regional, state, and local committees. More recently, the proliferation of manpower programs, many utilizing the same state and local agencies and drawing upon the same clientele, led the Labor Department to initiate the Cooperative Area Manpower Planning System (CAMPS).

Manpower Advisory Committees

The advisory committees were designed to involve management, labor, and other interest groups in the establishment of training policy and the determination of training needs. The National Committee has proved to be of modest effectiveness. It has been a useful sounding board for policies under consideration and has also made its own proposals for change. However, its independence and range of activities have been somewhat restricted because its staff is provided by the Labor Department and its agendas are approved by the Manpower Administrator. Its subcommittees have made useful studies and recommendations on various aspects of program operation such as the research program, the quality of the counseling provided under MDTA, and the need for coordination among manpower programs.

By and large, the eight regional committees have not been able to carve out a role for themselves. They parallel the regional structure of the BES and BAT, which was put together more for transportation and communications convenience than for homogeneity of economic interest. Since policy is not made on a regional basis, nor are programs administered by region, the regional committees can make no significant decisions which will affect either state and local projects or national policies.

The state and local manpower advisory committees are potentially more significant. All states have them, though individual ones occasionally lapse into inactivity, and there are well over a thousand local committees of widely varying activity. The assigned duties of the state committees are (1) to act as a liaison with the National Manpower Advisory Committee; (2) to interpret the national manpower programs for state governors and their staffs; (3) to promote public support for manpower training; (4) to promote the overall state manpower programs; and (5) to advise local manpower advisory committees. The local committees are expected (1) to help assess the present and future economic needs and manpower problems of the area; (2) to obtain commitments from employers to hire trainees; (3) to publicize MDTA; (4) to recommend training programs; and (5) to examine and evaluate proposals for training courses.

There is no direct contact between the state and national committees. A few state committees have a formal liaison with the governor's office, but it is probable that most governors are not aware of their existence. Few states have formal manpower plans, and, where they do, the state committees, which have no staffs, must rely upon the personal knowledge of their members in evaluating them. Although some state committees have played an active role in the development of an overall state plan, the guidance they provide for local committees appears to be almost negligible.

The experiences of local committees are similar. Limited by the time they can devote and lacking an independent staff, committee members can only examine and react to forecasts of future economic needs and manpower problems supplied by the local state employment service staff. Numerous cases can be found in which individual committee members have had a significant influence on local employers, but, over all, the contribution of the committees to placement appears negligible.

On the other hand, both state and local manpower advisory committees appear anxious to play a role in reviewing and making recommendations on specific training projects. Representing management, labor, or minority group interests, they not only feel knowledgeable and qualified but have a direct concern. There are regular meetings and good attendance early in the fiscal year when funds are available, and disinterest after funds are totally committed.

However, the program administrators prefer to limit the role of the state and local committees to discussing and recommending overall policy—lean programs for the many versus enriched programs for the few, the amount of basic education to be provided, or the occupational emphasis. The prospect of advisory committees, dividing along partisan lines and kibitzing on the proposal, approval, and operation of specific projects, is not an attractive one to them. A USES directive reads as follows:

> It should be clearly understood by all members that the committee may act only as an advisory body. . . . [It] does not have the authority to require or to veto the establishment of training programs. . . . where a majority of the members of a manpower advisory committee do not agree with the action of a state agency on a proposed training project . . . reasons for disagreement should be documented and signed [and] forwarded to appropriate BES regional office.

The final decision, however, is a federal one. The functions of the committees are greatly affected by the balance in interest and membership among various groups. Chairmanship is supposed to rest with public members, but at times a partisan member is appointed and, more often, the chairman's task falls by default to a state employment service official. Either by default or by virtue of his personality, some committees are dominated by a special-interest representative. The committees are directed to include minority group representatives as members, but this directive is frequently neglected. Where minority representation is present, the frequent result is healthy protests that minority group enrollment in programs is inadequate or that minority group members are being trained for jobs with substandard pay or undesirable working conditions.

A few committees have made significant policy contributions. For instance, the Detroit committee was instrumental in establishment of the skill center in that community. For the most part, however, the manpower advisory committees provide a protest mechanism, but not a formal veto, for aggrieved interest groups. It is not true that a *de facto* veto does not exist; for instance, organized labor in California was able to limit the first few years of the training program almost completely to jobs for women. The existence of the advisory committees probably made little difference in that case, but it appears to be rare for a state agency to fund a project against the advice of a state or local committee.

The experience with the MDTA advisory committees is typical of such committees throughout vocational education, apprenticeship, and training programs.[3] Where they have the interest and take the time, they make a difference, but apart from defending partisan interests, they rarely do so.

Cooperative Area Manpower Planning System

Coordination of federal manpower programs had become a major issue by 1966. By then, in addition to MDTA, the Economic Opportunity Act (EOA) had added the Job Corps, the Neighborhood Youth Corps, the Work Experience and Training Program, the manpower components of the Community Action Program, and the New Careers, Operation Mainstream, and Special Impact programs. Vocational education and vocational rehabilitation had been expanded, and both the specialists in vocational programs and the United States Employment Service were being pressured to serve a more disadvantaged population. Federal agencies were competing for local clientele, and local agencies were confronted with an increasing proliferation of federal programs and funding sources.[4]

At the same time, vocational educators continued to be restive at the degree of federal, and particularly Labor Department, control of the program. In addition, they found the

---

[3] Samuel M. Burt, *Industry and Vocational-Technical Education* (New York: McGraw-Hill Book Company, 1967).

[4] Sar A. Levitan and Garth L. Mangum, *Making Sense of Federal Manpower Policy*, Policy Papers in Human Resources and Industrial Relations no. 2 (Ann Arbor, Mich.: Institute of Labor and Industrial Relations, University of Michigan, 1967).

lapses of time between completion of one project and funding of another troublesome in terms of continuity of staff and facilities. Many in the Labor Department, on the other hand, considered the project-by-project approach vital to maintaining a flexible program constantly in touch with labor market conditions.

In implementing the amendment granting to the states review and approval authority for small projects, a state plan concept was developed providing guidelines for the states to use in their advance planning of the projects. Each state plan would require federal approval, but, once approved, the states could initiate individual projects throughout the year without further federal involvement.

The state plan for the small contracts appealed to the Manpower Administrator so much that he proposed its use for the total program. A conference of all involved agencies was held in September, 1965, to discuss the proposal, and a decision was reached to inaugurate it for fiscal 1967. However, no indication of the size of the 1967 program was available until after the President's budget message in January, 1966. Then decisions had to be made in the Labor Department and negotiated with HEW. By the time that federal guidelines were disseminated, state administrators had less than a month to prepare a proposal for the following year.

The state employment services were to exercise leadership in the planning process, but they were also to involve all interested agencies and to assure coordination with other programs. The haste required brought protests from agencies which claimed that they had been bypassed, but with the existence in most states of manpower coordinating committees composed of state employment service and vocational education officials, the institutional portions of the plans were reasonably good. OJT planning was much more difficult, and the planning machinery was much less developed. Planning proceeded in an air of unreality, since no one knew how much

Congress would choose to appropriate for fiscal 1967, and when. In fact, appropriations were not forthcoming until October, more than three months after the beginning of the fiscal year. Nevertheless, an even more involved planning process was envisioned for fiscal 1968.

The overlapping manpower and poverty programs had brought demands for either coordination or consolidation to a high pitch by the end of 1966. Thirteen three-man teams representing Labor, HEW, and OEO were in the field in thirty-two cities, attempting to cajole competing local agencies into cooperation. Legislative proposals to consolidate many of the programs were in the air.[5]

In that environment, and building on the first year's MDTA state plan experience, the Manpower Administration won approval from HEW, OEO, the Department of Commerce, and the Department of Housing and Urban Development for a Cooperative Area Manpower Planning System. The system was to consist of area, state, and regional coordinating committees. Final approval of state and regional plans as well as individual projects would remain the prerogative of the individual federal agencies. The CAMPS agreement was reached on March 3, 1967, after several months of negotiation. Guidelines were developed and sent to the states early in April. Local CAMPS committees were to formulate joint programs, sending them to the state for approval. The area plans were then to be consolidated into state plans in time for regional approval by July 1st.

Few of the states met the deadline, but most had their CAMPS plans in, and at least provisionally approved, before the end of the first quarter of fiscal 1968. All were completed before 1968 appropriations cleared the Congress in November. The quality of the results was uneven. Some of the plans showed evidence of careful thought. Other CAMPS commit-

[5] Levitan and Mangum, *Making Sense of Federal Manpower Policy.*

tees apparently understood neither the instructions nor the purpose of the exercise. Cooperation was surprisingly good, but, given the limitations of budgetary restrictions and the nature of the various programs, the area plans are better described as individual agency plans stapled together than as comprehensive planning documents shaped to local needs.

An effective planning system is still a long way off, but the experience thus far is promising. The core is the state employment services and the planning of MDT institutional projects. Because of the dependence on employers, OJT is more difficult for the agencies to plan. Economic Opportunity Act programs are funded by grants and contracts throughout the year as long as money lasts, and the Office of Education staff lacks the political leverage and the temperament to delay or withhold funds. To date, only the Labor Department appears sufficiently committed to refuse to release funds until appropriate planning is completed and approved.

The situation is difficult for state and local MDT authorities. In various locations, even though MDT planning was completed, their funds have been held up, pending the submission of plans by local EOA-funded agencies. On the other hand, no pressure on communities and states is available other than the withholding of money.

Complaints of the costs and administrative burdens of the CAMPS operation are growing, and it will probably be necessary for the federal agencies to earmark money for a supporting staff. The state and local committees complain that the Labor Department itself violated the spirit of CAMPS by introducing programs into the slums of large cities without consulting them. Stronger commitment will have to be won from the other federal agencies. The quality of current planning leaves much to be desired. The fact that planning must occur prior to the fiscal year, while funds may not be appropriated until its first quarter is past, is a continual problem.

Negotiations are currently under way to bring the Departments of Agriculture and Defense and the Civil Service Commission under the CAMPS umbrella. The stresses and strains are many, but if pressure for local and state involvement is maintained, staff is provided, and CAMPS plans are honored at the federal level, a useful planning and coordinating mechanism should result.

4:

Contributions and Costs of Manpower Development and Training

A total of $1.6 billion had been appropriated for training the unemployed and underemployed under Title II of MDTA through fiscal 1968 (Table 4–1). Although the Secretary of Labor and the Secretary of HEW have reported annually to Congress and a few cost-benefit studies have been made for samples of trainees, no independent *general* evaluation of the program is available. This appraisal of Title II, the manpower development and training (MDT) portion of the Act, was designed to fill that gap. The program has its strengths and its weaknesses. There are unresolved issues the appropriate solutions to which are by no means clear. But the overall contributions of the program have exceeded its costs by a margin which not only merits support but justifies expansion. This favorable conclusion is supported by an identification of

Table 4–1
MDTA Title II Funding

	Fiscal Year					
	1963	1964	1965	1966	1967	1968
	(thousands of dollars)					
Funds Appropriated	57,500	109,000	347,884	365,158	347,000	337,500
Funds Obligated	57,389[a]	108,552[b]	345,747[c]	364,982	346,710	—

[a] Includes $2,922,778 for 18 E & D projects.
[b] Includes $6,067,563 for 45 E & D projects.
[c] Includes $15,445,154 for 94 E & D projects and $1,298,832 for 17 Mobility projects.

the program's objectives, an appraisal of its accomplishments, and a comparison of its contributions with its costs.

OBJECTIVES OF MANPOWER
DEVELOPMENT AND TRAINING

The Manpower Development and Training Act's Statement of Findings and Purpose in 1962 listed goals ranging from insuring against the burdens of automation to "staffing freedom." Despite the verbiage, it is clear that the training program was originally designed to retrain experienced adult heads of families displaced from established jobs by technological and economic change. As the employment picture brightened, the targets changed, first to youths and then to other groups facing disadvantages in competing for existing jobs. These changes made MDTA an element in the antipoverty strategy. In addition to its primary objective of solving unemployment, tightening labor markets and inflationary pressures in 1966 led to enunciation of an additional goal— alleviation of labor shortages. Although it was never explicitly designed for the purpose, MDT has also become a lever for changing traditional manpower and educational institutions. In retrospect, these changing objectives can be justified by the original language of the Act. Another goal originally mentioned—the general upgrading of the labor force—has never become an explicit objective in practice.

Thus, as a result of original intent and subsequent experience, MDT has come to have six potential identifiable objectives: (1) facilitating employment of the unemployed; (2) providing an escape from poverty; (3) alleviating inflationary pressures; (4) meeting labor shortages; (5) upgrading the labor force; and (6) revamping traditional institutions.

Adequate evaluation of the Title II contributions requires not only an assessment of the extent to which the program as a whole has fulfilled its objectives but also of the degree to which its various components have contributed to those objectives. The first can be done, but the second requires information which is unavailable at present. Given the limitations of the data and concepts, cost-benefit analyses are most useful to corroborate judgments based on detailed examination of both quantifiable and nonquantifiable accomplishments. In this chapter I shall examine the extent to which each objective has been achieved and estimate the overall costs of the program before turning to a review of cost-benefit studies for comparison with previous conclusions.

REDUCING UNEMPLOYMENT

General Levels of Unemployment

MDT was confronted at its inception with a nagging conceptual problem. It made sense to retrain and re-employ experienced workers who had demonstrated their commitment to the work force and their productivity. They were substantial members of their communities with obligations which would suffer from their lack of employment and income. Their skills and abilities might deteriorate, thus precipitating them into a state of permanent economic dependence. However, there are only two ways in which a retraining program can reduce the level of unemployment, as contrasted with facilitating the employment of particular individuals: (1) the unemployed worker can be trained for a job which would otherwise remain vacant, or (2) employers can be motivated by the availability of trained labor to undertake activities they would otherwise have foregone. If, however, the result of training is only to shift the burden of unemployment from the trainees to those who would otherwise obtain available jobs, little has been accomplished.

The responsiveness of employment to fiscal stimuli during and since 1964 indicates that inadequacy of demand, not availability of skills, is the effective restraint on economic activity. Yet MDT trainees who completed their training in 1963 experienced a level of placement success almost as high as that achieved in the tighter labor markets of 1966 and 1967. Had the program trained a million persons by mid-1965, as its authors expected, the lack of job openings might have been a serious constraint.[1] As it was, there were sufficient openings in an economy providing over 70 million jobs to absorb the little more than 200,000 persons who had actually completed training by the end of that year.

This does not mean, however, that the jobs would not have been filled by others had the MDT trainees not been available. Labor shortages were primarily in two categories: (1) jobs requiring substantial training or skill and (2) unattractive low-wage jobs with a high turnover. MDT courses, which limited training to fifty-two weeks and averaged twenty-three weeks through 1963, could not contribute significant numbers of workers to the former category, and lack of skill and training was not the deterrent in the latter.[2] It is unlikely that many of the jobs filled by MDT completers in 1963 and most of 1964 would have remained vacant. Before the program could increase to a size sufficient to have an appreciable displacement effect, however, the 1964 and 1965 tax cuts had been passed and the Vietnam escalation was under way.

The MDT program was incapable of making a measurable contribution to the reduction of general unemployment. It was fortuitous that the complex task of establishing a remedial training system was still in its early stages when aggressive fiscal policies were adopted in early 1964. MDT trainees may have been given a competitive advantage over others who might have obtained the same jobs, even in the tighter labor

---

[1] U.S., Congress, Senate, *Congressional Record,* 87th Cong., 1st sess., 1961, 107, pt. 12:16797; and 87th Cong., 2d sess., 1962, 108, pt. 3:3673.

[2] Sar A. Levitan, *Federal Manpower Policies and Programs To Combat Unemployment* (Kalamazoo, Mich.: The W. E. Upjohn Institute for Employment Research, 1964), p. 16.

markets of 1965–1967. However, it is doubtful that displacement was appreciable because only 463,400 had completed training by the end of September, 1967. Since employment was expanding during most of the period, it is unlikely that MDT seriously worsened the competitive position of those who did not receive training.

Employing the Unemployed

The justification for a program to retrain unemployed workers in a slack labor market might be questioned, though it might also be argued that the underskilled should be helped to compete more effectively for whatever jobs are available. However, once the objective of training the unemployed was established by legislation, the test of administrative effectiveness was not the justification for the goal but the degree to which it was achieved. Since the accomplishment of all other objectives depends upon the extent to which participants find jobs, the best test of the program's success is its employment rates. Since the characteristics of the trainees and their post-training experience differ markedly for institutional and for on-the-job training components, it is useful to consider the two separately.

A. Post-Training Experience of Institutional Trainees. From September, 1962 through September, 1967, 601,000 persons had enrolled in institutional training projects. Of those, 346,700 had completed training and 74,000 were still enrolled, representing a dropout rate of 30 percent. Data obtained from three-, six-, and twelve-month follow-up surveys conducted by the United States Employment Service show that 90 percent of the institutional completers obtained employment at some time during the first year after training and that 77 percent were employed when last contacted. Three-quarters of those employed at the time of last contact (58 percent of all completers) considered their jobs to be training-related.[3] Of those not employed at last contact in 1966, about one-third, mostly women, were out of the labor force, with the remaining two-thirds unemployed. The stability of employment following training is the most significant measure of training success. Data are available for only 37,600 persons who had completed training prior to April 30, 1965, of whom 72 percent were employed 75 percent or more of the time within the first year following training (Table 4–2).

MDT's contribution to employing the unemployed can be assessed only by a comparison of post-training experience with what would have happened in the absence of training. Comparison with pre-training employment experience provides an indication, but since employment trends have been upward that approach is less than satisfactory. The proportion of institutional enrollees who had been either employed or unemployed for fourteen weeks or less immediately before entering training varied from 52 percent in 1963 to 60 percent in 1966 (Table 4–4). Many may have experienced more than one short period of unemployment during the twelve months prior to enrollment and some may have spent time outside the labor force. However, this is a reasonable estimate of those employed at least three-quarters of the pretraining year. When compared with the 72 percent employed at least three-quarters of the post-training year, the apparent 30 percent improvement in

---

[3] The proportion in training-related jobs had risen to 62.5 percent in 1966. The significance of the difference between training-related and non-training-related employment is difficult to ascertain. Since training related-ness was judged by the employee, there may be a conservative bias to the data. Enrollment by itself may have increased the visibility and desirability of the employee, thus contributing to his employability in nontraining-related jobs. However, only 11 percent of the employers interviewed in a 1965 evaluation study by the Labor Department reported they had hired trainees specifically because of their MDT training, and 77 percent of those hiring trainees for nontraining-related jobs thought people without training would have been as useful to the company as those hired. There appeared to be no conspicuous differences in the characteristics of those obtaining training-related and those obtaining nontraining-related jobs. The only significant findings were that those with training-related jobs tended to be better satisfied with their jobs and less likely to leave them.

Table 4–2
*Stability of Employment of MDTA Institutional Trainees,
through April, 1966*

Characteristics and Employment Status at Last Contact	No. of Reports	Percentage of Trainees Employed in Year Following Training Percentage of year employed			
		0–24	25–49	50–74	75–100
Total, All Categories	37,600	7	8	13	72
Employed	31,200	2	5	11	82
Unemployed	4,000	28	22	25	25
Out of labor force	2,400	32	24	22	22
White					
Employed	22,800	2	4	10	83
Unemployed	2,600	26	22	26	27
Out of labor force	1,800	31	24	23	22
Total	27,200	6	7	13	74
Nonwhite					
Employed	6,600	4	6	13	77
Unemployed	1,200	33	23	23	22
Out of labor force	400	32	25	23	20
Total	8,200	9	10	15	66

NOTE: percentages may not add to 100 because of rounding.

employment stability is significant, though it is in part attributable to general improvements in employment conditions as well as to MDT participation.

A more dependable approach for determining the employment contribution of the MDT program would be to compare the post-training employment experience of those who completed the program with the experience of comparable control groups who were not trained. In a study conducted for the Labor Department, the National Opinion Research Center (NORC) surveyed a nationwide sample of 784 completers and 413 dropouts from MDT institutional courses ending between June 1, 1964, and February 28, 1965. The control group was made up of 925 friends, neighbors, and relatives of the trainees who were also unemployed at the time that the trainees began training.

The difference in employment rates for the two groups before training was not statistically significant, but the post-training employment experience of the trainees was substantially more favorable than that of the control group. When interviewed, 68 percent of the completers and 41 percent of the controls had full-time jobs. An estimated 86 percent of completers and 64 percent of controls had been employed at some time during the post-training period. The completers had been unemployed on an average of 57 percent of the time during the year before training but were unemployed on an average of only 33 percent of the time during the post-training period. During the same years, the controls were unemployed 62 percent and 51 percent of the time, respectively. Both completers and controls appear to have experienced considerable unemployment, but those trained were clearly better off than those who had not received training. Participation in MDT was concluded to have increased post-training employment rates when compared to the control group—they ranged between 13 percent and 23 percent for the completers and 7 percent and 19 percent for the dropouts, depending upon the basis on which the rate is computed.

No general information is available on the 30 percent of institutional enrollees who failed to complete training. However, unpublished sample studies by the Department of Labor provide some insight. A 1965 study of 600 institutional dropouts in twenty-one cities, for instance, found that approximately one-third had left the program to take jobs. Another third left because they were dissatisfied with some aspect of the training, and the final third withdrew for a variety of family, health, and financial reasons.

MDT personnel argue that many of those who dropped out for jobs should be counted as successes rather than failures because they received adequate training and moved into jobs as soon as they were prepared. However, with limited information on their jobs, they remain outside the employment measures. Most of the dropouts occurred in the early weeks of courses, but the longer the course the higher the dropout rate. Those who dropped out tended to be from the more mobile groups. Young white males predominated among those leaving to take jobs, with nonwhite males dropping out for financial reasons. Those dissatisfied were largely young whites and those who were either new entrants or re-entrants to the labor force or who had had a high job turnover and a short duration of unemployment before enrolling. Most of those who dropped out for health and family reasons were female. The completers were somewhat more likely to be nonwhite and to have had longer unemployment and less successful labor market experience before entering training.

This study was corroborated by a similar survey a few months later, which found that 43 percent of the dropouts left to take a job or for financial reasons, 22 percent for health or family reasons, 19 percent because they were dissatisfied, and 7 percent because of transportation problems.[4] The Labor Department-NORC data and other studies suggest that the dropouts do tend to gain from their MDT participation, though they gain less than the completers.

B. Post-Training Employment of On-the-Job Trainees. Only 225,000 persons had been enrolled in on-the-job training as of the end of September, 1967. Of these, 116,700 had completed training and 62,000 were still in training, suggesting an OJT dropout rate of 20 percent. However, the meaning of the OJT dropout rate is less clear than for institutional training, since it includes either quitting or losing a job rather than a simple withdrawal from training. When last contacted, nine out of ten of those who had completed on-the-job training under MDT had either been retained by the contracting em-

---

[4] Similar results were found in a survey of similar size but limited to West Virginia trainees under the Area Redevelopment Act in 1963. See Gerald G. Somers, "Retraining: An Evaluation," in *Employment Policy and the Labor Market*, ed. Arthur M. Ross (Berkeley: University of California Press, 1965), pp 280–86.

ployers or had other jobs. The 8 percent who were in non-training-related jobs may be an indication of the latter.

No controlled study has ever been made to assess the extent to which those employed through MDT-OJT would have been employed in the absence of that program. Two crucial questions remain unanswered. The major difficulty arises because MDT support is available for on-the-job training of current employees as well as for the unemployed. Over all, 35 percent of OJT trainees were underemployed rather than unemployed or out of the labor force before training, and there has been no tendency for this proportion to decline. Presumably, most were already employed by the training employer. The second difficulty arises because with a tightening labor market many employers were seeking employees and training them when necessary. Under those circumstances it is difficult to judge whether MDT-OJT resulted in a net increase in training and employment.

Serving the Competitively Disadvantaged

The finding that MDT completers had a substantially more favorable post-training employment experience than a comparable group without training is evidence that the training was a benefit to them. It does not automatically justify the training program as a social investment, however, because it is possible that the trainees obtained jobs which would otherwise have been filled by others. Lacking empirical evidence, it is reasonable to assume that some substitution may have occurred in the slack labor markets of 1963 and 1964 but that very little occurred in the tighter ones of 1966 and 1967, with 1965 as a period of transition between the two situations.

However, there are circumstances where training is of social value even if substitution occurs. The changing structure of unemployment over time suggests that the labor market acts as an efficient selection mechanism, employing the best prepared first and leaving behind, whatever the level of employment, those with less to offer. Since the hiring process is largely employer-controlled, the system also lends itself to discrimination should employers choose to reject for noneconomic reasons those least attractive to them. The rising employment following the 1964 tax cut gave a more than proportionate share of the new jobs to most of those groups who had borne a disproportionate share of unemployment. Yet despite the increase in jobs unemployment remained concentrated by age, race, and sex, as well as by education, location, skill, experience, and occupation. Once unemployment rates stabilized, the flow of new jobs to the more favored groups resumed.

Unemployment has always shown a similar structure, though both demand conditions and demographic factors affect the relative burdens of various groups. What is new is a recognition of the problem and a commitment to alleviating it, even with low general levels of unemployment. The factors responsible for the increased sensitivity to individual and group unemployment problems are largely the product of two developments: (1) the debates over structural vs. aggregate demand explanations for persistently high levels of unemployment in the early 1960's, and (2) continued unrest among Negroes and other minority groups.

A consequence has been acceptance of the principle that improvement of the competitive position of those facing handicaps in seeking jobs is an appropriate goal for public policy, even though it may threaten those more favorably situated. Therefore, guidelines were issued in early 1966 directing that 65 percent of MDT trainees during fiscal 1967 should be drawn from the disadvantaged groups, as defined in Table 4–3. The remaining 35 percent of the training slots were to be used to reduce labor shortages, though the two objectives were not mutually exclusive.

Achievement of this goal for fiscal 1967 was not the significant development. As Table 4–3 shows, the goal as defined was close to realization when it was announced, but the cate-

Table 4-3

Program Goals for Fiscal 1967 Compared with Enrollments for Calendar Year 1966

Characteristics[a]	FY 1967 Goal (disadvantaged as proportion of all trainees[a])	CY 1966 Enrollments Institutional	OJT
	(in percentages)		
Age			
Under 22 years	23.5	38	35
Over 44 years	22.6	11	10
Nonwhite	20.4	40	24
High School Not Completed	49.3	54	43
Rural	12.8	18	22
Unemployed 15 Weeks and Over	30.0	40	32

[a] As chosen by the Labor Department Manpower Administration planning staff.

gories were so broad as to be of little significance as indicators of the degree of disadvantage, although there is a tendency for the competitively disadvantaged to be concentrated among those categories. Year-by-year trends in MDT enrollment for groups which have a high probability of job-seeking disadvantage are more meaningful indicators of progress. These trends are mixed, with institutional training enrolling more and more of those most disadvantaged but with OJT enrollments showing no such progress.

A. *Institutional Enrollments.* In the first years of MDT, when the Act was aimed at experienced, unemployed adults, of whom there were many, the program was admittedly "creaming."[5] As labor markets tightened, institutional enrollments moved steadily in favor of most, but not all, of those groups still burdened by high unemployment. As Table 4–4 indicates, the change in institutional enrollments has favored the

[5] Seymour L. Wolfbein, "The First Year of the Manpower Act," in *Unemployment and the American Economy*, ed. Arthur M. Ross (New York: John Wiley & Sons, Inc., 1964), p. 67.

nonwhite, the worker with nine to eleven years of education, the public assistance recipient, and the handicapped. The declining proportion of long-term unemployed is a consequence of falling unemployment. The nonwhite and those with nine to eleven years of education have been more than proportionately represented in institutional training when compared with their numbers among the unemployed. Those with eight years of education or less and those aged forty-five and over have been under-represented, and there has been little progress in their favor over the years.

Even with these commendable trends, the state employment service recruitment procedures tend to favor the most experienced and motivated among the disadvantaged. Outreach efforts through the Community Action Program's neighborhood centers and the USES Youth Opportunity Centers and Human Resource Development Program are increasing, but most MDT enrollees are still those with sufficient knowledge, experience, and motivation to seek assistance.

Administrators were slow to take advantage of the 1963 amendments authorizing basic education. Techniques and materials were limited, and few people were available who had experience in teaching basic education to adults. Despite the authorization, verbally oriented tests and local employment service practices and policies continued to impede enrollment of those with limited education. Some selection and referral officers tend to screen "from the top down," filling classes with the best qualified persons available. Some appear to have individual rules of thumb as to the minimum education necessary for successful training. Less than 5 percent of the more than 50,000 institutional completers in 1964 received basic education, but the proportion rose to 16 percent in 1965 and to 26 percent in 1966. Nevertheless, considering their high proportion among the unemployed, those with an eighth grade education or less remain seriously under-represented in institutional training.

Table 4-4

Comparison of Year-to-Year Trends in MDT Trainee Characteristics with Characteristics of the Unemployed

Characteristics	Year					Characteristics of Unemployed, 1966	
	1963	1964	1965	1966	1967[a]	Annual average	15 weeks and over
			(in percentages)				
Total Enrollments							
Institutional	58,400	102,500	140,900	162,500	118,900		
OJT	3,600	14,100	32,200	67,800	107,100		
Aged 21 Years or Less							
Institutional	31	40	43	38	39	n.a.	n.a.
OJT	36	32	45	35	37		
Aged 45 Years or More							
Institutional	10	10	10	11	11	25	39
OJT	7	10	10	10	10		
Education							
8 years or less							
Institutional	11	18	18	17	17	30	38
OJT	12	14	17	14	13		
9–11 years							
Institutional	31	33	35	37	40	27	29
OJT	29	28	32	29	30		

Nonwhite							
Institutional	27	31	35	40	42	22	24
OJT	15	24	28	24	27	—	19
Unemployed 15 Weeks or Over							
Institutional	48	46	44	40	42		
OJT	39	32	37	32	31		
Public Assistance Recipients							
Institutional	9	10	11	11	12	n.a.	n.a.
OJT	2	3	4	2	3		
Handicapped							
Institutional	6	7	8	9	10	n.a.	n.a.
OJT	4	5	5	4	5		

[a] Through September, 1967.

B. OJT Enrollments. As pointed out earlier, the enrollment of disadvantaged persons in OJT is inherently difficult.
Not only is their proportion in OJT low, but there is no evidence of improvement (Table 4–4). The OJT program is
authorized to upgrade the underemployed, and over one-third
of OJT trainees enrolled in 1967 were in that category. The
theory is that the upgrading will open entry positions to the
disadvantaged, but there is no administrative control over
selection of those to be trained or those for whom entry
jobs are to be made available. The difficulty of controlling
enrollments under the current administrative structure is indicated by the fact that in 1965 79 percent of trainees covered
by contracts directly administered by BAT or state apprenticeship agencies were drawn from the ranks of the unemployed, while only 43 percent of those under community contracts with community action agencies, the Urban League, and
similar organizations were unemployed when they entered
training. Only 25 percent of the trainees in programs of national contractors (mostly trade associations) did not already
have jobs.

C. Coupled Programs. Given the fact that both on-the-job
and classroom training methods have their advantages and
disadvantages, the reasonable strategy is to couple them wher-
ever possible. To a limited extent, vocational education has
followed this procedure through "cooperative programs" between schools and employers. Apprenticeship has done so to
a greater degree through related classroom instruction. Among
the MDT goals for fiscal 1967 was the funding of sufficient
coupled projects to provide training opportunities for 72,500
persons.

The results were disappointing. By the end of fiscal 1967,
though the number of regular OJT "slots" authorized had
risen to 98,100 as compared to 132,300 for the institutional
component, coupled programs had been approved for only

54,600 trainees. There were several obstacles. Apprenticeship and training personnel had little use for institutional training, while vocational educators doubted that OJT even merited the title of "training." The former group attempted to minimize the amount of time spent in institutional preparation, while the latter argued for extending it.

In addition, the coupling system contemplated a contract with an employer to accept particular trainees in specified numbers at the end of the institutional training phase. Since employers were reluctant to make this commitment, permission was given to enroll trainees in institutional courses on the assumption that OJT "slots" could be contracted for upon completion. However, the few projects which so far have completed the institutional phase have an OJT placement rate no greater than that for regular institutional courses. In some cases, for reasons as yet not clear, the dropout rate in the OJT phase exceeded that in the institutional period. Extraordinary efforts were made to expand the number of coupled projects, including insistence that all OJT contracts made in the last few months of fiscal 1967 and the first months of fiscal 1968 include coupling. As already noted, the MA-1 projects which resulted from disappointment with the coupling approach have as yet been no more impressive.

Employing the Disadvantaged

The test for MDT is not only whether it enrolls the disadvantaged in training, though that in itself is a contribution, but whether they are employed after training.

A. Employment of Disadvantaged Institutional Trainees. As might be expected, post-training employment and unemployment rates vary widely by trainee characteristic. In 1966 one-fourth of all nonwhite institutional completers were unemployed at last contact as compared with 14 percent of white completers (Table 4–5). Only 66 percent of the nonwhite

Table 4–5
Post-Training Labor Force Status of MDT Completers,
by Trainee Characteristic, 1966

| Characteristic | Employment Status at Last Contact | | | |
	Training-related employment	Non-training-related employment	Unemployed	Not in labor force
	(in percentages)			
Institutional				
Sex				
Male	62.1	17.6	15.6	3.7
Female	62.9	7.5	18.7	9.9
Color				
White	65.7	12.4	14.0	7.0
Nonwhite	55.1	13.3	24.3	6.1
Age				
Under 22	60.3	13.6	18.0	7.1
Over 44	53.4	12.3	18.4	9.8
Education				
8 years or less	51.8	16.3	24.3	6.4
9 to 11 years	59.0	14.2	19.1	6.6
12 years or more	66.6	10.9	14.6	7.0
Enrolled in courses including basic education and prevocational training	55.0	15.1	21.7	7.4
Total	62.5	12.5	17.2	6.8
On-the-Job				
Sex				
Male	92.6	3.4	2.2	1.1
Female	85.4	1.9	7.8	4.4
Color				
White	90.7	3.1	3.7	1.9
Nonwhite	89.3	2.4	5.4	2.4
Age				
Under 22	88.9	3.3	4.0	3.5
Over 44	91.3	1.2	3.5	1.7
Education				
8 years or less	82.8	4.0	9.6	2.5
9 to 11 years	89.4	3.0	4.6	2.1
12 years or more	92.0	2.8	2.8	2.0
Total	90.6	3.0	3.8	2.0

NOTE: percentages do not add to 100 because of nonreporting of training-relatedness.

institutional trainees were employed at least 75 percent of the time during the first year following training as compared with 74 percent of white completers (Table 4–2). The percentage of nonwhites employed was significantly lower than whites even when controlled for age, education, occupation, and duration of pretraining unemployment. The relationship between employment rates of those with eight years or less of education and those with twelve years or more was similar to that between nonwhite and white completers. Only 70 percent of those under 22 years of age and 66 percent of those over forty-four years were employed during at least three-quarters of the first year after training as compared with the figure for all trainees of 72 percent.

Those who had completed courses involving basic education and prevocational training in 1966 experienced a disappointingly high unemployment rate. However, they did somewhat better than those with eight years of education or less, who were probably heavily represented in the basic education courses. The number completing courses involving basic education was double the number with eight years or less of education, suggesting a substantial involvement of those trainees with nine to eleven years of schooling. Studies are needed to ascertain whether basic education under MDT has made a significant difference in employment rates, but logic and experience support a strong presumption that it has.

Nine out of ten institutional completers obtain jobs, but they apparently continue to have considerable instability in employment. This is not surprising in view of the fact that only a little over half of the labor force works full time for the full year and MDT completers during the first year after training typically face "last in-first out" problems.[6] However, the unemployment rate of the institutional completer is much lower than it would have been in the absence of training. It

---

[6] Forrest A. Bogan and Thomas E. Swanstrom, "Work Experience of the Population," *Monthly Labor Review* (December, 1966), p. 1370.

is also not surprising, though it is disheartening, that the incidence of unemployment is higher for those completers drawn from various disadvantaged groups than for the group as a whole.

The Labor Department-NORC data show employment gains by age, race, sex, and education, with females and whites benefiting more than their opposites but with gains roughly equal for all education groups and most age groups. Thus the indications are that, bad as the post-training employment experience of some of the disadvantaged groups has been, their experience in the absence of training would have been worse.

B. *Employment of Disadvantaged On-the-Job Trainees.* The employment experience by trainee characteristic for OJT completers is impressive and offsets to a substantial extent the disappointing OJT enrollments among the disadvantaged. Since enrollment in OJT includes employment, the question is whether the trainee is retained by the employer after his training is completed. More than one-third of OJT trainees were already employed before entering training, but the program made important contributions to the employment experience of the remainder. Even if it is assumed that all of the 6 percent of OJT completers who were unemployed when last contacted after training in 1966 were drawn from those who were unemployed before enrolling in OJT, the employment rate for that group when last contacted still exceeds 90 percent. Differences in employment and unemployment rates of OJT completers on the basis of color are insignificant and those based on age are minor. Differences based on sex and education are significant, but the variation is much less than for institutional trainees and, what is more important, the differences occur at a much higher employment level.

If only the average costs per trainee are considered, OJT appears to be the least-cost means within MDT of employing the disadvantaged. For example, a Negro in 1966 had only about one-half the likelihood of getting an available OJT "slot" that he had of getting an available institutional one. Once in OJT, however, his likelihood of post-training employment was 34 percent higher than it would have been had he been institutionally trained, and the cost of training him averaged only one-fourth as much.

There are other considerations, however. It is likely that the OJT trainees are less disadvantaged within each category than those enrolled in institutional courses. Also, in the longer run, in institutional training the broader selection of skills taught and the inclusion of basic education, if this is done, may contribute enough to employability and promotability to offset the immediate OJT advantages. No one will know whether this is so until long-term follow-up studies are made. A more important issue is whether those in OJT would have been trained at the employer's expense in the absence of the program. However, the value of OJT to those less attractive to employers is undoubtedly high.

C. Analysis by Race. Because of the particular significance of the problems of unemployment among Negroes, it is useful to compare MDT participation and results by race, by state, and by region. In all states, the proportion of nonwhite enrollment in institutional courses has exceeded the proportion of nonwhites in the 1960 population, in most cases by multiples of two to five.[7] In southern states the proportion of nonwhites in institutional training has tended to be almost double that in the population as a whole. The number of nonwhites in OJT has been considerably below that in institutional training but has still been considerably above their proportion in the popu-

---

[7] For data to support this analysis, see "Manpower Programs in the Anti-poverty Effort," in Examination of the War on Poverty, Staff and Consultant Reports, prepared for the Senate Committee on Labor and Public Welfare Subcommittee on Employment, Manpower and Poverty by Garth L. Mangum (Washington, D.C.: U.S. Government Printing Office, 1967), vol. 2.

lation except in the South, where nonwhites have tended to be at or below their level in the population.

Data on training occupations and employment by state for OJT are unavailable because of under-reporting. Though nonwhite persons appear to get their share of institutional slots, there is evidence of an unfavorable selection process in the occupations for which Negroes are trained. Nonwhite trainees have been under-represented, compared to their total enrollment, in training for professional and technical and skilled occupations; they have been proportionately represented in clerical and sales and semiskilled occupations; and they have been over-represented in service occupations. There has been a clear tendency for both white and nonwhite trainees to be upgraded away from unskilled, agricultural, and service jobs through training for skilled, clerical, sales, professional, and technical jobs. Under-representation of nonwhites in training for professional-technical and skilled jobs tends to widen the racial gap in those occupations. At the same time, MDT's overall impact is probably to narrow the gap as nonwhites exit from service jobs and enter semiskilled and clerical occupations more rapidly than white trainees.

There seem to be no consistent regional departures from the national pattern. Certain southern states have greater under-representation of nonwhites in professional and technical jobs than the national average, but at least as many states outside the South can be found with equal under-representation in clerical and sales occupations and over-representation in service and semiskilled occupations. Mississippi is the only southern state consistently below the national norm for every occupational group but one, yet Mississippi and Louisiana have trained whites and nonwhites for skilled occupations at three times the national rate.

Placement experience of nonwhites is much less positive than the picture of nonwhite enrollments, as already noted. The same pattern is evident in all but a few states, but the margin between white and nonwhite placements has been widest in the South. There appears to be considerable bias in OJT enrollments and none in institutional enrollments. The reasons for these differences between white and nonewhite enrollments and placements are unclear. Whatever the reasons, the problem is a national one, only slightly more serious in the southern states. Though there is no bias in national MDT policies, there is a national responsibility to identify the reasons for the significant racial differences in the program's operation.

CONTRIBUTIONS TO THE ANTIPOVERTY EFFORT

Family income has not been considered a relevant statistic for the MDT reporting system. However, covered earnings data from Old-Age, Survivors, Disability and Health Insurance (OASDHI) records and data from the Labor Department-NORC study provide indications of pre- and post-training incomes of MDT trainees. From these sources it would appear that at least one-half of MDT institutional trainees, and a lesser proportion of the smaller number of OJT trainees, have been from families whose incomes were below the poverty line.

Income measures of poverty vary by family size and location, but such refinements are not available for OASDHI data. However, an annual income of $3,000 is a reasonable working figure. As Table 4–6 shows, 81 percent of institutional trainees and 50 percent of on-the-job trainees who were heads of families trained in 1966 had covered earnings of less than $3,000 for the last full year before entering training. As might be expected, the proportion of low incomes was highest where the family head was female, or nonwhite, or under twenty-two or over forty-four years of age, or with limited education. Data for earlier years indicate a similar pattern.

Family income would probably exceed the covered earn-

Table 4-6

Characteristics of 1966 MDT Trainee Heads of Families[a]
by CASDHI Annual Earnings Status

	Annual Earnings			Percent of Total under $3,000[b]
Training and Characteristics	Below $3,000	Above $3,000	None Reported	
Institutional				
Sex				
Male	31,400	15,100	9,700	73.2
Female	17,500	2,100	13,500	93.7
Color				
White	28,000	12,500	12,500	76.4
Nonwhite	20,900	4,700	10,700	87.3
Age				
Under 22	10,400	1,100	3,500	92.7
Over 44	6,300	2,400	4,200	81.4
Education				
8 years or less	9,500	2,600	4,900	84.7
9 to 11 years	19,500	6,000	9,000	82.6
12 years or more	19,900	8,600	9,300	77.2
Total	48,900	17,200	23,200	80.7
On-the-Job				
Sex				
Male	10,700	16,800	3,300	45.5
Female	1,900	300	1,200	91.2
Color				
White	9,300	15,200	3,300	45.3
Nonwhite	3,300	1,900	1,200	70.3
Age				
Under 22	3,300	1,700	900	71.2
Over 44	1,300	2,400	700	45.5
Education				
8 years or less	1,800	2,200	700	53.2
9 to 11 years	3,400	4,300	1,200	51.7
12 years or more	7,400	10,600	2,600	48.5
Total	12,600	17,100	4,500	50.3

[a] Annual covered earnings data from Social Security Administration records. A random selection was made of 80,000 records using the last digit of the enrollee's Social Security number. The sample was inflated by a weighting process to represent total enrollment for the year and was characterized by family status. Separate sampling ratios were developed for institutional and OJT training. Earnings are for the last full year prior to training.
[b] Includes those with no reported earnings.

ings of individual heads of families because of other wage earners in the family, noncovered employment, and transfer payments such as unemployment insurance. In the Labor Department-NORC survey 53 percent of the institutional trainees whose training ended between June 1, 1964, and February 28, 1965, reported that their family income just prior to training was less than $60 a week, which would amount to $3,120 for full-year employment. However, most families of trainees experienced considerable unemployment as well. One-third reported family incomes of less than $40 a week, and three-fourths reported less than $100 a week.

The MDT program's success can be evaluated in part by its ability to raise these low incomes. Table 4–7 shows that

Table 4–7

Changes in Earnings of MDT Completers from Year prior to Enrollment to Year after Completion of Training[a]

Enrollment Year and Characteristic	Institutional Training			On-the-Job Training		
	In- crease	No change[b]	De- crease	In- crease	No change	De- crease
	(in percentages)					
1965						
Heads of families earning less than $3,000	70	8	22	66	10	24
Heads of families earning more than $3,000	28	21	51	44	20	36
Non-heads of families	71	6	23	66	9	25
Total	64	9	27	60	12	28
1964						
Heads of families earning less than $3,000	79	4	16	82	7	11
Heads of families earning more than $3,000	35	29	36	37	41	22
Non-heads of families	78	6	16	76	13	11
Total	71	9	20	76	13	11
1963						
Heads of families earning less than $3,000	72	8	20	77	6	17
Heads of families earning more than $3,000	30	24	46	33	39	27
Non-heads of families	73	6	21	71	10	19
Total	64	10	26	62	17	21

[a] Includes only those who had covered earnings in both periods.
[b] Plus or minus 10 percent represents no change.
NOTE: percentages may not add to 100 because of rounding.

the majority of trainees with low pretraining earnings had higher earnings after training than would have been expected on the basis of the mere passage of time. This was also true of non-heads of families. On the other hand, most of the heads of families with covered earnings of more than $3,000 experienced either no significant change or a decrease in earnings for the year after training. The latter were more likely to be individuals with substantial skills and seniority who had to start at the bottom of the ladder in new jobs following training.

The same pattern is apparent in the straight-time hourly earnings of those completers who were employed at last contact (Table 4–8). As of January 30, 1967, the median pretraining hourly wage of all employed completers was $1.44. The median post-training hourly wage was $1.74. As with annual covered earnings, those trainees with low initial earnings appear to have profited more in terms of income than those with high pretraining earnings. Both pre- and post-

Table 4–8

Straight-time Average Hourly Earnings of Employed Completers, Pre- and Post-Training,[a] September, 1962–January, 1967

Straight-Time Average Hourly Earnings	Total		Whites		Nonwhites	
	Pre-training	Post-training	Pre-training	Post-training	Pre-training	Post-training
	(in percentages)					
$0.50–$0.74	7	2	5	1	10	3
0.75–1.14	21	8	19	6	27	12
1.15–1.24	4	2	4	2	5	3
1.25–1.49	23	21	23	20	26	25
1.50–1.74	14	17	15	18	12	16
1.75–1.99	8	13	9	13	6	13
2.00–2.49	12	20	13	22	8	16
2.50–2.99	6	11	7	12	4	8
3.00 and over	4	6	5	6	2	3
Total	100	100	100	100	100	100
Median	$1.44	$1.74	$1.48	$1.80	$1.32	$1.60

[a] Last regular employment prior to training and at time of last post-training contact.

NOTE: percentages do not add to 100 because of rounding.

training medians were lower for nonwhite trainees, but the percentage increases were almost identical. A similar pattern prevailed for non-heads of families as compared to heads of families and for females relative to males.

It is significant that whereas almost one-third of the trainees who completed training had earned less than $1.25 an hour in their last regular employment, only 12 percent earned less than $1.25 an hour after training. Fifty-five percent of the completers had pretraining earnings below $1.50 per hour, as compared with only one-third whose post-training earnings were below that level. Most trainees who earned less than $1.25 an hour after training were in service occupations: many were nurses' aides and ward attendants, and significant numbers were in clerical and sales jobs and in agriculture. However, 5 percent of those in skilled categories made less than $1.15 an hour after training, and one-fifth earned less than $1.50 an hour. Among women 47 percent earned less than $1.50 per hour after training, as compared to 21 percent of male trainees, while 43 percent of nonwhites and 29 percent of whites were in the same low wage category.[8] One might question the propriety of training for jobs with such low earnings, and, in fact, an administrative decision has been made not to train workers for jobs paying less than the federal minimum wage. However, there is no assurance that follow-up studies of employed trainees will not find them working at lower wages than might be expected.

In spite of the fact that many persons are left with low earnings after training, the median earnings for both whites and nonwhites were 21 percent higher after training, which represents a greater increase than could be expected from the normal upward movement of wages, considering that the average length of the training period was little more than half a year. Those with higher pretraining earnings probably also

[8] Mangum, "Manpower Programs in the Antipoverty Effort," p. 319.

had higher post-training earnings than would have been the case in the absence of training. Data from the Labor Department-NORC study show that the average weekly earnings of the completers, which had been 9 percent below those of the controls, increased after training to about the same level as those of the employed controls. The study also corroborated the finding that the greatest wage increases went to those with the lowest pretraining wages.

Though MDT has made a significant contribution to the income of its enrollees, its contribution to the overall reduction of poverty is too small to be significant. It is gratifying that in five years perhaps 250,000 low-income persons, half of whom were probably heads of families, have been helped to raise their incomes, most probably from just below the poverty line to a little above it, particularly when compared with the experiences of other programs. However, with 9 million poor families in the United States, the dent made by MDT programs is hardly noticeable.

LABOR SHORTAGES AND INFLATION

Since training does not in itself create jobs, MDT cannot be expected to have a significant impact on general levels of unemployment. It is conceivable, however, that MDT could play an important role in a full employment policy by reducing the inflationary consequences of any given level of employment and unemployment.

Manpower Programs and Inflation

One rationale for the manpower programs of the 1960's had been that, though they could not create jobs, they could lower the trade-off rates between unemployment and inflation, allowing general demand policies to lower the unemployment rate with fewer inflationary consequences.[9] It ap-

9 Garth L. Mangum, "The Role of 'Job Creation' Programs," in *Unemployment in a Prosperous Economy*, ed. William G. Bowen and Frederick H. Harbison (Princeton, N.J.: Princeton University Press, 1965), p. 407.

peared logical that training programs could reduce the labor shortages which contribute to production bottlenecks and shortages of goods and services. Better recruitment procedures, placement services, and relocation assistance could help allocate and re-allocate the available labor supply more quickly and smoothly. Less skilled workers could be made more attractive through basic education, work attitudes, and skill training, this reducing employer competition for workers with experience and skills. Those with the greatest competitive handicaps could be hired directly by public programs or subsidized in private employment, again devices to reduce unemployment with the least inflationary impact on the economy.

MDT's potential contribution is considerable. Training unemployed workers to fill available jobs should be a direct link between reducing unemployment and preventing labor shortages. The OJT program could function as a subsidy to reduce employer reluctance to hire the disadvantaged. However, even if this thesis were demonstrable, any contribution from a program which has trained less than 500,000 persons in five years could not be of measureable importance in a labor market of 85 million workers. Even if the antipoverty work and training programs are considered as well as MDT, an average of only 300,000 persons were involved full time, year round, in 1967, with another 200,000 participating in summer programs. The total contribution may have been significant, but it is certainly not substantial or measurable.

The only policy measures to have a real impact on the employment and income of disadvantaged groups were the tax cuts of 1964 and 1965, followed by the less consciously planned but equally effective escalation of the Vietnam war. Further reductions in the general level of unemployment would have an even greater relative impact because fewer nondisadvantaged workers would have to be absorbed first. The assumption that training and other manpower programs can be effective in restraining price increases and thus lessen unemployment appears to have widespread support.[10] Political efforts to expand such programs to meaningful size have not followed from this assumption, however.

MDT and Labor Shortages

The MDT program was designed to serve the unemployed, not the labor market. It has trained not for occupations with labor shortages but for those with a "reasonable expectation of employment." The difference is a philosophical one of "ends vs. means," but it has important practical consequences. The primary objective of MDT is to facilitate employment, and eliminating labor shortages in given skills is secondary. Therefore, USES personnel are directed to identify not only shortages but also occupations in which high turnover, numerous retirements, or expectation of expansion will provide job opportunities. In allocating 35 percent of the MDT effort to the alleviation of skill shortages, occupations whose members are in short supply nationally were listed and it was suggested that attention be given to them in setting up training projects.

At one extreme, the occupations most likely to experience critical shortages of labor are those requiring training time beyond the two-year legislative limit and the one-year practical limit of MDT. The new authority to provide refresher training for registered nurses and other "out of touch" professions is the only significant potential contribution at the professional-technical level, and experience is insufficient to assess its results.

At the other extreme, occupations such as those of nurse's aide, hospital orderly, food service attendant, and custodian constantly suffer labor shortages either because of low wages or bad working conditions. Turnover in such jobs is high and demand continuous. Most of those trained for such occupations could probably have obtained the jobs without training,

---

[10] *Economic Report of the President* (Washington, D.C.: U.S. Government Printing Office, 1967), pp. 100–13.

but the program serves as a recruitment and placement mechanism. Such training without provision for upgrading the job as well as the worker probably to some extent restrains the already weak economic forces pressuring for wage increases.

Between these two extremes is a group of reasonably attractive occupations in which there is an almost constant demand for labor—for example, those of machinist, automobile mechanic, welder, and stenographer. A few, such as drafting and licensed practical nursing, are at higher levels but still within MDT's purview. In addition, preapprentice and other entry level training for jobs requiring additional training and experience can be and has been supplied by MDT.

The best measure of the extent to which MDT trains for occupations in relatively short supply is probably its relationship to state employment service unfilled job orders. Though these job orders account for only about one-third of the local job vacancies, their occupational distribution closely resembles actual labor market conditions.[11] As Table 4–9 shows, the MDT occupational distribution has not correlated well

Table 4–9

Occupational Distribution, Institutional MDTA Courses and Employment Service Unfilled Job Orders

Occupational Group	Unfilled Orders, June 1, 1967	Estimated MDTA Enrollment, FY 1967
	(*in percentages*)	
Professional, Managerial, and Technical	34	12
Clerical and Sales	17	21
Service	15	17
Machine Trades	12	21
Bench Workers	7	6
Structural Workers	8	18

NOTE: percentages do not add to 100 because some occupations have been excluded.

[11] U.S., Congress, Joint Economic Committee, Subcommittee on Economic Statistics, *Hearings, Job Vacancy Statistics*, 89th Cong., 2d sess., 1967, p. 156.

with the distribution of unfilled orders, but enrollments have been so few relative to total demand that surplus trainees have rarely, if ever, been produced.

Institutional training is credited with having placed in occupations with labor shortages 31 percent of its trainees in 1965 and 34 percent in 1966. Comparable OJT figures are 15 percent and 20 percent, respectively.[12] However, the only occupations involving as many as 5 percent of total institutional enrollments through September of 1966 were those of licensed practical nurse, nurses' aide and orderly, clerk-typist, stenographer, automobile mechanic, welder, and general machine operator. Proportionate enrollments for OJT were limited to nurses' aides, orderlies, and aircraft sub-assemblers. With the possible exception of licensed practical nurses, it is probably more accurate to say that in training for occupations with a reasonable expectation of employment, and considering the relatively short training periods and restricted per trainee expenditure, MDT does supply workers with skills locally demanded but not in critically short supply.

Upgrading the Labor Force

Every training effort adds to the total supply of skills available. The contribution to the labor force of this general upgrading process depends upon the degree to which the skills provided are relevant, durable, and transferable to other uses. A major strength of MDT is its direct relevance to short-run labor market expectations. Training is limited to jobs for which there is current demand. In fact a problem has been the tendency of some state employment service personnel to be too bearish about job openings. An offsetting weakness of most immediate relevance is the questionable durability and transferability of some of the skills for which training is provided. Because of the income needs of the individual and the desire

---

[12] *Manpower Report of the President* (Washington, D.C.: U.S. Government Printing Office, 1966), p. 156.

to minimize costs per trainee, the emphasis is on the shortest possible route to an immediate job. Institutional training is probably broader in content than OJT but is generally more restricted than regular vocational education.

The inclusion of basic education in institutional training is probably the single most significant contribution to upgrading of the labor force. However, it has been limited because it lengthens courses and raises costs. The 1966 amendments to MDTA authorized teaching of communications skills. These ancillary efforts need not be relevant to training for specific skills but increase the trainee's general employability. However, the individual, not the labor force, is still the focus. MDT results in significant upgrading of the relatively small proportion of the labor force involved, but this is a bonus, not a primary objective.

REORIENTING INSTITUTIONS

One important contribution of the manpower development and training program was unforeseen. Most of MDTA's architects saw it as an attack on unemployment. A few people involved in early amendments to the Act saw in it a potential means of bringing the disadvantaged into the mainstream of the economy.[13] Even they recognized only after the fact two more modest but still significant effects: (1) the reorientation of two major labor market institutions—the federal-state employment services and the vocational education system, and (2) the significant modification of union and employer policies.

Impact on the Federal-State Employment Services

As earlier noted, MDT caught the USES in the midst of a reorientation quite different in emphasis from that which would characterize the 1963–1967 period. With added funds

---

[13] Curtis C. Aller, "The Role of Government-Sponsored Training and Retraining Programs," in *Unemployment in a Prosperous Economy.*

which had become available in 1961 and 1962, USES activities were being centralized in downtown offices in metropolitan areas. New and refurbished buildings were being provided to escape the "unemployment office" image. Offices were becoming specialized along occupational lines, with particular attention to the rapidly growing white-collar fields. Services to employers were emphasized, and placements were the measure of performance.

USES participation in training under the Area Redevelopment Act was the first step in another new direction. Although involvement in various antipoverty efforts has accelerated the move toward new objectives, MDT has been the most important force for change. Before MDTA USES could offer little hope or help to an applicant who lacked the skills to fit the job orders on file. MDT required identifying occupations with "reasonable expectation of employment" and screening the unemployed for their suitability for training. It changed the question "Does he have the skill?" to "Can he acquire the skill?"

As the MDT emphasis shifted to youth, the USES directed the opening of 140 Youth Opportunity Centers throughout the nation. Negro unemployment and training needs put the spotlight on the racial practices of some state employment services. Special projects were launched to supply counselors to handle the new MDT load. In dealing with the disadvantaged, inherent biases in testing techniques were identified. National publicity and pressure for a good MDT placement record encouraged active development of job opportunities to fit an applicant's abilities and needs.

Subsequently, the Employment Service has become involved in recruiting for the Job Corps and Neighborhood Youth Corps, stationing personnel in poverty program neighborhood centers to serve the poor and in military induction centers to serve Selective Service rejectees.[14] Inertia and resistance from

---

[14] Mangum,"Manpower Programs in the Antipoverty Effort."

personnel on both federal and state levels have delayed change. Yet progress is indicated by the current Human Resource Development emphasis which is designed to change the Employment Service philosophy from that of a "screening out" to that of a "screening in" agency.[15]

Impact on Vocational Education

The impact of MDTA on vocational educators has been even greater than on the employment services. Since employment services are state-run with full federal financing, they are accustomed to working within, though they often subvert, federal guidelines. However, the federal role in vocational education has been limited to the provision of matching grants and the determination of broad occupational groupings within which funds may be spent. Even the G.I. Bill merely provided funds to be used at the discretion of the states and the schools. Vocational education enrollments were overwhelmingly concentrated in the areas of agriculture and home economics, with the emphasis on programs at the high school level. Adult enrollment was almost completely made up of employed workers interested in upgrading their skills, and there were few opportunities for the high school dropout. In some parts of the country segregated facilities either offered no opportunity to minority groups or limited the occupations to which they had access. Efforts to improve the image of vocational education tended in the direction of raising entrance requirements, thus ruling out those most in need of help.[16]

MDT provided full federal financing but insisted on federal project approval. State officials considered budget allocations

[15] Frank H. Cassell, "Management of the U.S. Employment Service," mimeographed (Paper presented to a USES staff meeting, Washington, D.C., September 6, 1966).

[16] U.S., Department of Heath, Education, and Welfare, Office of Education, *Education for Employment, Highlights and Recommendations from the Report of the Advisory Council on Vocational Education* (Washington, D.C.: U.S. Government Printing Office, 1968).

to be sacrosanct, but federal MDT officials did not hesitate to re-allocate uncommitted funds to states exhausting their allocations. Vocational educators complained of excessive paperwork and complex reporting procedures. Federal control was resented, and overburdened facilities required overtime operation to handle MDT requirements. The General Accounting Office insisted upon an eight-hour day, in contrast to the more customary six hours. The project-by-project process made recruiting and maintaining a staff difficult. Federal policies interfered with local racial practices.

Many of these problems remain, but accommodations have been made and a workable program has emerged. State employment service and vocational education personnel have learned to work together and, in many cases, to enjoy the contact. School principals have discovered a source of materials and equipment which, though primarily for MDT purposes, can often be used for regular courses as well. Where a school had invested in facilities and equipment, there was once a tendency to continue a course regardless of need. Federal MDT officials have encouraged flexibility and have required movement of equipment among schools within a state as community needs vary. Most important of all, vocational educators have learned to serve effectively and to be concerned about the welfare of a disadvantaged population. In doing so, new institutions and techniques, including multioccupational projects, skill centers, and the provision of prevocational and preapprenticeship training and basic education, were developed and refined. As Table 4–10 indicates, the population served by the skill centers is a consistently more disadvantaged one than that served by other MDT projects in the same community. Data from these centers show 94 percent of trainees receiving basic education, with almost 50 percent receiving over 600 hours of course instruction.

Most MDT instructors were hired from industry, but many, including most of the administrative staff, had been vocational

Table 4–10

Characteristics of Persons Enrolled in Selected Skill Centers Compared with Those of Persons Enrolled in Control Projects in the Same Labor Areas[a]

Trainee Characteristics	Skill Centers	Control Projects
	(*in percentages*)	
Males	72	36
Age		
Under 22	41	25
Over 44	9	14
Education		
8 years or less	24	5
9–11 years	41	30
12 years or more	35	65
Nonwhites	55	40
Unemployed	86	69
Unemployed 15 Weeks or More Before Training	49	47
Public Assistance Recipients	16	14
Handicapped	9	7
Total enrollees	3,960	8,634

[a] The characteristics of 1967 enrollees in 11 skill centers were compared with those of enrollees in control projects in the same occupations and labor markets. For comparisons by skill center and labor market, see Garth L. Mangum, *Contributions and Costs of Manpower Development and Training*, Policy Papers in Human Resources and Industrial Relations no. 5 (Ann Arbor: Institute of Labor and Industrial Relations, University of Michigan, 1967).

educators. Freed from many institutional constraints and assigned to a particular clientele with more generous equipment and staffing budgets, these vocational educators showed substantial innovative ability. In addition to developing new curricula and new methods of integrating basic education with skill training, several worked out modular approaches to training. Acceptance of new trainees, either on an individual basis or in groups, at frequent intervals during the training period rather than only at the beginning, was made possible.

As other manpower programs have been launched, the skill centers have provided a vehicle for the Economic Opportunity Act's Adult Basic Education and Work Experience and Training programs. One of the MDT skill centers run by vocational educators has become a residential school and provides a useful comparison with the Job Corps Urban Centers. The Mahoning Valley Vocational School, located on a partially deactivated air force base, is completely financed by MDT and serves about 400 youths (aged sixteen to twenty-one) from all over Ohio. Since MDT does not provide for residential facilities, the trainees pay for their housing with their subsistence allowances. The trainees are encouraged to maintain their family and community ties and to return home on weekends.

Several significant lessons can be drawn from this experience. (1) Despite the frugality enforced by the absence of funds for residential, medical, and related purposes, costs per student amount to $6,500 if calculated on a fifty-two-week basis and $6,200 if calculated on a forty-eight-week year. Job Corps costs of about $8,000 have been widely criticized as excessive.[17] The Mahoning Valley comparison suggests the inevitable costliness of residential programs. (2) The encouragement of frequent home visits by the Mahoning Valley School is contrary to the original Job Corps preference for putting as much distance as possible between the trainee and his home environment. Whether the practice accounts for the relatively low (35 percent) dropout rate, in contrast to the Job Corps experience, is a matter for speculation. (3) The educational establishment of a reasonably progressive state can serve the seriously disadvantaged if it is given a specific assignment to do so. (4) There is a need for residential training facilities to serve a scattered population, those with no homes, or those with unsatisfactory home environments. The Mahoning Valley School has already attracted the interest of the Appalachian Regional Commission and the Vocational Education Advisory Council. It was also one of the bases for the 1967 Proposal of Congressmen Albert H. Quie and Charles E. Goodell that the Job Corps be transferred to the

[17] Levitan, *Antipoverty Work and Training Efforts*, pp. 24–29.

public schools. Mahoning Valley may prove a useful pilot project for the development of residential schools. In the meantime, the 1967 EOA amendments directed the establishment of nonresidential training centers modeled upon the MDT skill centers. Why Congress felt that the underutilized skill centers could not themselves be made available is unclear.

Thus far the changes in clientele and developments in training techniques mentioned above have been limited to MDT projects, for the most part. However, these projects are run by vocational educators and operate within the school systems. Thus there are indications that at least some MDT practices will find more general adoption.

Impact on Apprenticeship

Apprenticeship as a traditional route to skilled craftsmanship has been increasingly criticized as an obstacle to the employment of minority groups, particularly Negroes. Despite the publicity given overt discrimination, the limited number of apprenticeship opportunities and inability to pass objective tests are the more formidable barriers. Though many have discriminated in selection of apprentices and few have worked aggressively to assure equal access to apprenticeship programs, unions have exerted the most pressure for expansion of apprenticeship opportunities. Since registered apprenticeships number about 200,000 at any one time, and there are about the same number of unregistered apprenticeships, they offer no overall solution to minority group employment problems; even so, their number exceeds the total enrollment in manpower programs.

Members of minority groups have little knowledge of apprenticeship opportunities, and few know craftsmen or union officials who can act as their advocates. Deficiencies in their education preclude their passing the increasingly technical entry exams, even when they surmount other barriers. The Workers Defense League in New York City, with the help of MDT funds, demonstrated the effectiveness of aggressive efforts to interest youths who either lacked information or did not consider apprenticeship a realistic possibility. In addition to coaching applicants for successful performance in qualifying examinations, WDL helped gain the support of employers and union leaders and provided a buffer for the latter vis-à-vis some of the less responsive union members.[18] With MDT funding the WDL effort is being extended to other cities.

Though limited in scope at present, preapprentice training developed under MDT has considerable potential. MDT funds can be used both as a subsidy to reduce employer reluctance to undertake apprenticeship training and as a source of education and training to prepare for entry into apprenticeship programs. By December 31, 1966, a total of 48,000 preapprentice-training slots had been approved.[19] Information on the results of these projects is limited, but the initial indications are promising.

The National Tool and Die and Precision Machinery Association reported that all but a few of its preapprenticeship trainees continued on to achieve apprentice status. Only 7 percent of the preapprentices were Negro, but even this figure was a step forward in a traditionally all-white industry. However, it is informally reported that a high proportion of these Negroes dropped out during the preapprentice phase. The association was particularly gratified that as a result of its MDT-OJT participation 35 percent of the small shops in the industry initiated apprenticeship for the first time. Similarly, Chrysler Corporation, though withdrawing from the MDT-OJT program because of "government red tape," reported that 550 of its dealers had been induced to start apprentice training, while

18 F. Ray Marshall and Vernon M. Briggs, Jr., *The Negro and Apprenticeship* (Baltimore: Johns Hopkins Press, 1967).
19 John S. McCauley, "Increasing Apprenticeship Opportunities through Pre-employment Training," in *Research in Apprenticeship Training* (Madison: Center for Studies in Vocational and Technical Education, University of Wisconsin, 1967), pp. 113–23.

the corporation itself intends to continue the program at its own expense. The American Hospital Association also reports the inauguration of permanent training programs in hospitals as a result of its initial MDT-OJT experience.

While about one-fifth of the preapprentices have been trained as machine operators, many of them in nonunion firms, the best indications of the potential leverage that MDT can exert on apprenticeship practices are provided by the projects involving the building trades unions. Contracts are current with the Carpenters, Bricklayers, Operating Plasterers, and Painters, as well as with the National Association of Home Builders. In many cases local union cooperation has been excellent, suggesting that ability to qualify has been the only obstacle to admission to these programs. In other cases where discrimination had been evident, national union support and the provision of "coaches" as advocates of minority youths have enabled significant numbers of applicants to circumvent overt obstacles. Although the numbers involved have been few, the preapprentice approach, if pursued aggressively, may ultimately have a substantial impact on apprenticeship practices.

COSTS OF MDTA

The financial accounting system of MDTA has been constructed with, as almost its sole object, the protection of public funds. This single focus results in a structure which makes the determination of the program's costs in relation to its benefits extraordinarily difficult. Expenditures are authorized for projects which are taught in several succeeding sections, each enrolling only a portion of the approved number of trainees. Reports on expenditures for training allowances are immediate, while actual training expenditures are reported only at the completion of the total project. Thus training expenditures cannot be related to any particular group of trainees, and at a project's end costs can only be divided by the total number of trainees enrolled. No information is available on comparative costs per training hour for various projects, trainees, occupations, and training methods. There is no point in time at which cumulative MDT expenditures can be determined and related to cumulative enrollments, completions, and employment experience. Instead, it is necessary to accept per trainee costs of completed projects as typical of the present as well as the past.

The problems are illustrated by the relationship between funding, expenditures, enrollments, and completions. Through September, 1967, about $1.3 billion had been committed for MDT projects, $1 billion for institutional programs and the remainder divided almost equally between OJT and coupled programs. This funding authorized training for 1.125 million persons, while only 826,000 were enrolled, of whom 463,400 were completers and 135,000 were still in training. The 227,600 unaccounted for were apparently dropouts, but the 299,000 difference between those enrolled and those for whom projects were funded is a peculiarity of the MDT financial system. Changes are currently under way the nature of which is less than clear. A description of the system which has prevailed up to this point will highlight some of the problems of estimating MDT costs.

MDT'S FINANCIAL SYSTEM

MDT's practice has been to obligate funds for an entire institutional project at the time of approval by the joint Labor-HEW regional review teams. Projects are to start within sixty days, but longer delays often occur. They may continue through several sections, the last of which is expected to (but often does not) begin within twelve months of approval. Projects are funded on the basis of estimated enrollments and costs per trainee. If either figure is overestimated or if trainees drop out too late to be replaced, unspent funds can be recovered and used in the second fiscal year. These practices confuse the relationship between funds, expenditures, and trainees.

OJT funds are committed when approved by the BAT in Washington. The shortfall between OJT project approval and funding and subsequent enrollments and expenditures is largely the result of overestimating the number of slots that the community contractors can fill. This is true even though some community contractors have filled slots far beyond the number authorized by their contracts, since even more contractors have fallen short of their quota. In addition, BAT personnel have not always had the time to check with employers to make sure that funded courses begin and continue. In some cases money has remained unspent because employers did not bill the agency for the reimbursement authorized by the contract.

Late in 1967 the MDT financial system was undergoing a drastic revision. Because of the delays and shortfalls in training, committed but unspent funds had begun to accumulate, and this situation attracted the attention of the Bureau of the Budget and the appropriations committees and constituted a threat to future budget approvals and appropriations. The issue came to a head in summer, 1967, when, in response to the riots, a survey was taken to determine how many ghetto residents were being served by MDT and how many slots were available. No appreciable amount of uncommitted funds existed, and there were few available training slots. Yet, as of June 30, 1967, $107 million of fiscal 1966 funds and $232 million of fiscal 1967 appropriations remained unspent.

The money was not in danger of being lost to MDT. In fact, much of the accumulation in the institutional sector of the program appeared to be the result of deliberate policy in several states, designed to get around what they considered administrative obstacles in the federal regulations. As is discussed further in Chapter 6 below, the project-by-project federal approval procedure often caused time lags between projects, resulting in loss of instructors and idle facilities. The uncertainties of the congressional appropriations process aggravate the problem. The proposing and winning approval of large multioccupational projects to be conducted in several sections guarantee continuity over a longer period. Ceilings had also been placed on costs per trainee in various regions in order to increase the number of trainees possible within given budgets. Equipment purchases were charged as current expenses to the initial project for which they were intended, rather than amortized over a number of subsequent projects. Several states also circumvented this obstacle by the multisectioned, multioccupational route. For example, in California, where costs per trainee were highest because of high training allowances, a ceiling of $4,000 per trainee was imposed. If equipment was included, a 1,000-trainee project might exceed this limit while a 4,000-trainee project that spread the cost over four sections would not.

Having discovered the accumulation of committed but unspent funds, federal officials stepped in to end the practice. Regulations imposed in late 1967 required funding of all projects in the first half of the fiscal year, beginning of all projects by the end of the third quarter of the year, and enrolling of the last trainee before the end of the year. Without special approval, funds committed but not spent within these limits will be withdrawn and committed elsewhere. A new reporting system requires monthly notification of training slots unfilled and money outstanding. These new regulations will not make calculation of costs any simpler. However, reasonable estimates can be made even with current data.

COST PER TRAINEE

Estimates of cost per trainee used for authorizing projects were 20 to 30 percent higher than actual costs in the early years of the program because of dropouts and because the administrative problems of overestimating were easier to handle than those of underestimating. Labor Department financial officers report that current estimated costs appear to be in line with the costs per trainee of completed projects and therefore are good approximations of actual cost per enrollment (Table 4–11). No data are available on cost per completer, but this can be estimated because 27 percent of all enrollees, cumulatively, have failed to complete their training courses.

The costs per trainee for institutional programs have risen over time in part because of the general upward trend in salaries and other costs, but primarily as a result of more generous training allowances, more liberal eligibility requirements, and longer courses. The average adult weekly training allowance has increased from $35 to $54, excluding the subsistence allowance paid to those training too far from their homes to commute, and the proportion receiving training allowances has risen from 60 percent in 1963 to about 85 per-

Table 4–11
*Estimated MDT Costs per Enrollee and per Completer,
Cumulative to September, 1967*

Training	Average Cost Per Enrollee		Estimated Cost Per Completer[a]
	To September 30, 1967	FY 1967	
Institutional	$1,540	$1,900	$2,000
Allowance costs		1,045	
Training costs		770	
Nonfederal costs[b]		85	
OJT[c]	405	380	485
Coupled	970	1,050	
Allowance costs[d]		255	
Training costs[d]		235	
Average Cost[e]	1,150	1,145	1,460

[a] Calculated by inflating costs per enrollee by the 27 percent noncompletion rate of the total program and the 30 percent and 20 percent noncompletion rates of the institutional and OJT segments, respectively.
[b] Total state cash contributions divided by total enrollments.
[c] Excludes coupled.
[d] Institutional phase only.
[e] Based on total MDT expenditures (institutional and OJT).

cent in 1967. Initially allowances accounted for one half of total institutional costs; they are now 60 percent of costs and are still rising.

As Table 4–12 shows, the length of the typical institutional course has been steadily growing. Another and closely related fact is that course hours per week have also increased from 1963, when two-thirds of the projects involved thirty hours or less per week, to the situation in fiscal 1967, where 80 percent of projects were scheduled for between thirty-six and forty hours weekly. The primary reasons for the increase in weeks were the 1963 authorization of an additional 20-week allowance to encourage basic education and an effort to limit short courses with little skill content. The 1965 amendment allowing training up to 104 weeks to handle teaching of technical skills has never been implemented, primarily because the higher per trainee costs involved would limit the total number of trainees. The added hours per week were brought about by a General Accounting Office decision that those receiving allowances should train on a normal work week basis rather than follow the customary school schedules.

Training allowances are paid in OJT projects only for supplementary off-the-job instruction, and these situations are rare outside of coupled programs. Excluding allowances, institutional training costs are twice as high as expenditures per

Table 4-12

Estimated Percent Distribution of Duration of MDT Institutional Training Activity

Duration of Projects	Fiscal Year				
	1963	1964	1965	1966	1967[a]
4 Weeks or Less	6.4	5.2	4.2	2.2	1.4
5–17 Weeks	28.0	24.0	28.2	18.7	18.0
18–26 Weeks	21.8	24.8	23.1	18.2	23.1
27–51 Weeks	43.7	45.3	44.2	52.5	53.1
52–72 Weeks	0.1	0.7	0.4	8.4	4.4

[a] Projects approved through December 31, 1966.
NOTE: percentages nay not add to 100 because of rounding.

trainee for OJT. In evaluating this fact, a number of other factors must be kept in mind. OJT expenditures are reimbursements negotiated with employers ostensibly to cover training costs. In practice, they may amount to more or less than the actual costs of the training. Therefore, they vary by the amount of actual training involved, the nature of the training, the willingness of the employer to pay for the training, the negotiating ability of the OJT administrator, and the administrative costs. The occupational structure is different, and the amount of training given during the hours spent on the job may vary widely. The primary factor in the reduction of OJT costs has been an attempt to keep the duration of OJT courses below 26 weeks. Costs of coupled programs are a combination of institutional and OJT costs and vary according to the mix.

VALIDITY OF TRAINING COSTS

The validity and appropriateness of training costs is difficult to determine without a detailed project-by-project study. Determination of eligibility for training allowances is a nondiscretionary matter determined by legislation and administrative guidelines. The increased generosity in allowances resulted from the identification of persons in need of training but blocked by financial obstacles. Since most such persons are unemployed heads of families and the majority are from low-income families, the likelihood of need for financial support is apparent.

An element of incentive is involved in the youth allowances and the still to be implemented provisions for allowances for part-time training of the employed. Many trainees could undoubtedly be supported by their families while training, though the additional income is welcome. However, since they are primarily dropouts who probably would not otherwise undertake training, the social benefits of integrating them into the work force have been considered worth the cost.

In the initial period, local vocational educators saw MDT as a way to obtain needed equipment not available through their existing budgets. When it became apparent that equipment costs were likely to become excessive, HEW officials tightened up on approval of training costs. As a result, equipment costs as a proportion of training costs fell from 25 percent in the earlier years to 8 percent in fiscal 1967. Rental of equipment was advocated where the need was temporary, and transfer of equipment from completed projects to others within the same state was required to reduce duplication of equipment purchases. The development of permanent centralized skill centers also helped to assure adequate amortization of equipment costs. From casual observation, it appears that MDT courses are better equipped than run-of-the-mill vocational courses, but there is no appearance of general excess. HEW officials also found it necessary to carefully review ratios of teachers to trainees and supervisors to instructors and other aspects of instructional costs. The ability to contract with private schools whenever the same training can be purchased more cheaply than in the public schools provides a useful control.

The more important cost considerations at present involve course content and occupation. The addition of basic education to the curriculum made it possible to train the functionally illiterate; it also added approximately $750 to the average training cost of those receiving it. Similarly, prevocational orientation to assist inexperienced trainees in making occupational choices takes weeks, and each week adds approximately $60 to the cost per trainee. Counseling is an expensive item. Individual referral, while important in isolated areas and to assure occupational choice, is also more expensive than regular institutional training.

Congress has been generous in granting Administration requests for liberalizing eligibility and broadening the scope of training, and has, in fact, added many features of its own. However, no additional funds have been provided to carry through these innovations. Therefore, as program content has been enriched, enrollment capability has been reduced. Since total funds are limited, the choice is between minimal training for more trainees and a richer offering for less. National officials and local employment services have tended to opt for the former. Vocational educators have tended to press for the latter. The desirable choice is by no means clear.

Institutional costs do not appear to be out of line with vocational education costs in general, and the possibility of competition from private training provides a yardstick for judging appropriateness of costs. The validity of OJT training costs must be determined ultimately by the actual training content and by the degree to which more or different training is given than the employer would have undertaken at his own expense. It also involves squarely facing the question of whether the pay is for training or for the right to influence the employer's hiring choices. Unfortunately, none of these questions has been answered by program administrators. BAT personnel were convinced that employers assume most of the OJT costs and that substantial increases in the amount and quality of training result, but no data were gathered to support that opinion.

COST-BENEFIT ANALYSES OF MANPOWER DEVELOPMENT AND TRAINING

As near as can be determined, some $675 million in federal funds had been spent through September, 1967, on the 463,-400 persons who had completed training by that date. The remaining $625 million of the total of $1.3 billion was allocated to the 135,000 still in training and the 300,000 not yet enrolled for whom training projects had been authorized.

The program made substantial contributions to the welfare of the individuals involved. The question left to be determined is the relationship between the benefits and the costs.

The MDT program has yet to be submitted to an overall cost-benefit study adequate in size, data, and concept to provide definitive results for the program as a whole. However, the results of the studies of MDT and related projects and the calculations based on total program data have been consistent enough, and the margins of benefits over costs have been sufficiently large, to leave little doubt that the program has been a good economic investment. The data on contributions and costs developed in this book are sufficient to allow a comparison and to corroborate those results.

The cost-benefit studies have been of two types: (1) those which compared the pretraining and post-training employment and earnings of samples of MDT trainees and estimated the time period necessary for them to repay the public investment in the form of higher earnings and tax payments, and (2) those which compared the post-training employment and earnings of those completing training with comparable control groups who were not trained. All of the MDT cost-benefit studies included costs to the trainee and the economy as well as the taxpayer. One study considered employer costs, though it is not necessary to include the latter to assure that the government got its money's worth.

A study of state-sponsored retraining in Massachusetts concluded that the savings in unemployment compensation alone would repay the training costs in a little over five years.[20] Studies of the experiences of 907 MDT trainees in the same state estimated that the public investment of $600,000 in training would return more than $4 million in benefits over the working life of the trainees.[21] A study by HEW based on a sample

[20] "Retraining the Unemployed," *New England Business Review,* April, 1963; reprinted in *Nation's Manpower Revolution,* pt. 2:608–27.

[21] David A. Page, *Retraining under the Manpower Development Act: A Cost-Benefit Analysis,* Brookings Institution Studies of Government Finance, Reprint 86 (Washington, D.C.: By the Institution, 1964).

of 12,700 trainees estimated a return in gross earnings of $2.24 per year for each dollar invested and repayment of training costs in five years from federal income taxes alone.[22]

Two more careful studies had the advantage of control groups: one of ARA-sponsored training in West Virginia found an average investment of $800 per trainee to bring a social return between $4,300 and $16,800, depending upon various assumptions concerning discount rates and relative private vs. social interest.[23] A study of 373 Connecticut workers trained in three occupations under MDTA concluded that the cost-benefit ratio for the average trainee was between three and six, and at least eleven for the government.[24] Follow-up studies of the Connecticut and West Virginia projects after five years found the advantages of trainees over controls still persisting.[25]

All of these studies were limited to institutional training. A more recent study, based on a sample of 2,000 institutional trainees and 650 OJT trainees, has attempted to assess the costs and benefits of the total Title II program.[26] While the ostensible purpose of the study was to develop and demonstrate methodology, and considerable reservations were ex-

[22] U.S., Department of Health, Education, and Welfare, Office of Education, *Education and Training—Third Annual Report on Training Activities* (Washington, D.C.: U.S. Government Printing Office, 1965).

[23] Gerald G. Somers and Ernst Stromsdorfer, "A Benefit-Cost Analysis of Manpower Retraining," *Proceedings of the Industrial Relations Research Association,* December, 1964; Glenn G. Cain and Ernst Stromsdorfer, "An Economic Evaluation of the Government Retraining of the Unemployed in West Virginia, 1965," mimeographed. See Gerald G. Somers, ed., *Retraining the Unemployed* (Madison: University of Wisconsin Press, 1968), for summaries of these and a number of related cost-benefit studies of retraining programs.

[24] Michael E. Borus, "The Economic Effectiveness of Retraining the Unemployed," *Yale Economic Essays,* 4, no. 2 (Fall, 1964): 371–429.

[25] M. Borus, "Time Trends in Benefits from Retraining in Connecticut," and Gerald G. Somers and Graehme H. McKechnie, "Vocational Retraining Programs for the Unemployed," in *Twentieth Annual Winter Proceedings of the Industrial Relations Research Association, Washington, D.C., December, 1967* (Madison: University of Wisconsin Press, 1968).

[26] Planning Research Corporation, *Cost Effectiveness Analysis of On-the-Job and Institutional Training Courses, A Report to the U.S. Department of Labor, Office of Manpower Policy, Evaluation, and Research* (Washington, D.C.: By the Corporation, 1967).

pressed concerning the available data, the sources were the same used throughout this study and the results merit consideration.

Pretraining and post-training employment and earnings experiences were compared. The average net federal benefit-cost ratio, including the direct and indirect benefits to society (exclusive of increased taxes paid), compared with the federal expenditure per trainee, was concluded to be 3.28:1 for OJT and 1.78:1 for institutional training, considering only net additional earnings of the first year after training. Calculations were made for all enrollees. The gains were taken as support for a working hypothesis that exposure to the labor market information and placement system through the training program was as important as the skills acquired. Using completers only, the ratios were 2.13:1 for OJT and 1.09:1 for institutional training. The calculations included an element of indirect savings in unemployment compensation, public assistance, and other costs of unemployment. The ratios of incremental earnings only to federal training costs were 1.98:1 and 1.62:1 for OJT trainees and completers, respectively, and 1.07:1 and 0.78:1 for institutional trainees and completers respectively. However, since the indirect benefits were significant and the benefits of training were almost certain to continue beyond the single year, it was considered that both forms of training were a desirable federal investment.

The institutional trainees had a more favorable benefit experience, primarily because they experienced more unemployment prior to training, though OJT trainees had higher wages and less unemployment after training. However, the higher institutional costs brought the federal-cost private-benefit ratio below the level of OJT. The authors of the study revised this conclusion by assuming that the OJT reimbursement was only one-half the actual cost of the training to the employer. By adding the assumed private training costs to the federal costs a negative first-year cost-benefit ratio was produced for OJT.

However, the assumption of additional employer costs was made on the basis of BAT judgment unsupported by data. A more valid assumption would be that, regardless of the extent to which he was reimbursed, the employer was getting his money's worth, and had at least expected to do so, when he signed an OJT contract. Otherwise, he would not have participated in the program. Therefore, any additional private costs were offset by the employer's private benefits and should be ignored in evaluating the returns to the public investment.

All these cost-benefit studies were plagued by difficulties of data and concept, most of which have been recognized by the authors. The relevant question is that of how the results of the training program differ from experience without it. Those studies lacking control groups leave to speculation the vital question of whether training is the relevant variable which explains the post-training gains. Control groups chosen from the ranks of those workers who did not seek training, were not offered training, or did not complete training were assumed to be comparable to groups from the same labor force population who sought and completed training. The probability was recognized that the trainees were more aggressive and likely to be more attractive to employers than were the controls. A really comparable control group is probably impossible to find, however, and all of the studies quoted seem weak in this regard.

Samples of trainees in particular locations and occupations are not necessarily typical of the entire program. The control studies involved only those trained in educational institutions. On-the-job training is lower in cost, but the problem of finding comparable control groups and determining the actual contribution and costs of OJT training is more difficult. The small-scale sample studies have the advantage of dependable data but the disadvantage that they may not be representative. Gross analyses are totally representative but require that vast assumptions be made to compensate for inadequate data. The information on pretraining employment and earnings is limited; the post-training follow-up surveys are a source of uneasiness because of their serious under-reporting.

With such rudimentary data and techniques, all conclusions on the basis of cost-benefit analyses should be treated with restrained skepticism. No quantitative study can measure the returns from reorienting the state employment services or vocational education. Regardless of arithmetic, an increase in the earnings of a white, thirty-five-year-old suburban high school graduate does not have the same social value as a similar increase accompanying the successful employment of a Negro or Mexican-American ghetto resident. The latter may be a good investment even if the additional earnings never repay the costs. Nevertheless, the consistency of the findings is reassuring.

Despite many reservations concerning the available data, simple calculations based on the evidence gathered for this report lead to conclusions similar to those of the cost-benefit studies. As indicated earlier, it seems that 30 percent more institutional trainees worked at least 75 percent of the weeks in the year following training than in the year before. If one-half the gain is attributed to rising economic activity, the results are not inconsistent with the conclusion of the Labor Department-NORC study, which suggests that MDTA institutional completers worked approximately 300 hours more in the first year after training than might have been expected in absence of the training. The median wage for all completers was $0.20 an hour higher than normal upward wage patterns would indicate. The resulting average addition to their annual incomes from the increased hours and the increased hourly pay for previous and additional hours would be in the neighborhood of $750.

Assuming these simple calculations to be valid, the first-year benefits of the institutional program would have to be maintained for two additional years to equal the costs of the program. There is no reason to think that OJT would not do as well for its previously unemployed trainees. Its impact on the incomes of the employed who are upgraded and the extent to which upgrading brings in others at the bottom remains uncertain. However, similar benefits would equal OJT costs per completer in less than a year.

The need for better data is obvious. More detailed analyses are needed to determine the worth and relative payoff of various aspects of the program. The relative effectiveness of institutional and on-the-job training is still in doubt. The returns from basic education need exploration. The costs and benefits for various trainee groups and for different occupations, training methods, and training institutions may vary. However, there appears to be little reason for doubting the value of the manpower development and training program in general. Its objectives have been justifiable social goals, and its benefits seem to have exceeded its costs by a substantial margin.

5:

Planning, Research, and Demonstration

THE manpower development and training program can be evaluated more or less objectively by examining its impact on the employment and earnings of its participants, supplemented by judgments concerning nonquantifiable contributions. Evaluation of the varied activities authorized by Title I of the Act is more difficult.

Title I, as originally written, reflected Senator Clark's concern for national manpower planning and the Labor Department's judgment that a retraining program would need a research base. The annual *Manpower Report of the President* is the only significant residual of the former concern. The research program has the potential not only for expanding knowledge of manpower problems and their solutions but also for attracting researchers and research institutions to a new area of effort. But the worth of research findings seldom can be assessed within a few short months or years of their publication, and the value of the augmented research manpower will depend upon its lifetime contributions.

An experimental and demonstration program was undertaken with Title II training funds and given permanence by transfer to Title I. Its potential contribution is great, but experiments may fail as well as succeed, and the success of demonstration programs can be measured only as they are adopted and adapted over time by operating programs. Along with the experimental and demonstration program, authorization for labor mobility demonstration projects and for an experimental guarantee of fidelity bonds was added to Title I.

The first plan is of sufficient interest to merit special treatment, while the second is discussed as part of the E & D program. Annual funding for these activities is shown in Table 5–1.

Table 5–1
Title I Funding

	Fiscal Year					
	1963	1964	1965	1966	1967	1968
	(*in thousands of dollars*)					
Total Allocations	825	2,100	2,100	29,000	24,000	23,400
Total Research	822	2,100	2,101	3,796	3,800	3,800
Contract research	822	2,100	2,101	2,669	2,602	2,600
Research grants				1,127	1,198	1,200
E & D	(2,923)ᵃ	(6,068)	(15,445)	19,990	14,941	15,000
Mobility Projects			(1,298)	4,995	4,969	4,400
Bonding				175	44	200

ᵃ Numbers in parentheses represent funds and projects from Title II budgets used for purposes which were later transferred by Congress to Title I. These sums are not included in totals.

Some concrete though nonquantifiable evidence is available to allow assessment of the current and potential contributions and problems of the Title I efforts. However, evaluation must rest primarily upon the judgments of an observer who has watched the administration of these activities in their formative years and is willing to speculate about their present and potential contributions.

MDTA IN A MANPOWER POLICY

Senator Clark's dream of manpower planning whose basis was at least as coherent and sound as that of economic planning has never been approached under MDTA or in the total complex of manpower programs. At first, the persistence of a high unemployment rate and subsequent recognition of the plight of the disadvantaged, even with tight labor markets, kept policy-makers' emphasis on employment as a source of income and status rather than on manpower as an economic resource. Further experience has proved the effectiveness of broader economic policy measures, but it has also introduced a certain modesty into expectations of forecasting ability and political wisdom. The complexities of labor markets are as great as those if any other portion of the economy when examined below aggregate levels. Finally, there are no tools of aggregate manpower policy other than general economic and educational policies. Yet below aggregate levels, the complexities of labor markets are too great to lend themselves to policy determination. On the other hand, MDTA and the plethora of similar acts have demonstrated the need for better coordination and long-range planning in federal manpower and related programs.[1] As was noted in Chapter 3 above, MDTA has had considerable impact on manpower planning at the state and local level, but it has been less influential in bringing about coordination at the federal level. It has, however, been instrumental in raising the general level of awareness of manpower issues.

The concerns reflected in the original Clark proposal were maintaining high levels of employment, forecasting manpower requirements, influencing occupational choices, and encouraging allocation of manpower according to socially desirable priorities. With the first year's experience under the Act, it became apparent that administrative coordination among federal agencies and bureaus and numerous state and local instrumentalities was a pressing issue. In a report issued in the spring of 1964, the Senate Subcommittee on Employment and Manpower recommended that "the Secretary of Labor should grasp the nettle of leadership even more firmly than in the past, both within his own Department and in coordinating manpower policy formulation and program administration throughout the federal government. Other departments and agencies should recognize this (Title I) mandate."[2] As one means of effectuating such coordination, a President's Com-

---

[1] See Levitan and Mangum, *Making Sense of Federal Manpower Policy.*

[2] U.S., Congress, Senate, Committee on Labor and Public Welfare, Subcommittee on Employment and Manpower, *Toward Full Employment, Proposals for a Comprehensive Employment and Manpower Policy in the United States,* 88th Cong., 2d sess., 1964, pp 42–43.

mittee on Manpower was created, chaired by the Secretary of Labor.

PRESIDENT'S COMMITTEE ON MANPOWER

Three quite divergent forces were pressing for the establishment of the President's Committee on Manpower, even though the legislative authority referred to in the Executive Order was Title I of MDTA. One was the continuing interest of the Senate subcommittee in encouraging manpower planning and coordination of manpower programs. The second was a special National Academy of Sciences Committee on the Utilization of Scientists and Engineering Manpower, which in a 1966 report had recommended the establishment of a White House Committee to coordinate scientific manpower interests.[3] The third was those members of the Labor Department staff interested in establishing their primacy in manpower policies and programs vis-à-vis challengers in HEW, the Council of Economic Advisers, and such high-talent, manpower-oriented executive agencies as the Office of Science and Technology, the National Science Foundation, the Atomic Energy Commission, and the National Aeronautics and Space Administration.

The language of the executive order designated the secretaries of Agriculture, Commerce, Defense, HEW, and Interior, the directors of the Bureau of the Budget, the NSF, the NASA Office of Emergency Planning and Selective Service System, and the chairmen of the Atomic Energy Commission, the Civil Service Commission, and the Council of Economic Advisers as members of the committee chaired by the Secretary of Labor to advise the latter in carrying out his Title I duties. However, the charter was written permissively enough for the

---

[3]*Toward Better Utilization of Scientific and Engineering Talent: A Program for Action* (Washington, D.C.: By the Academy, 1966).

Committee to pursue any manpower activity which did not conflict with an established interest.

It was soon apparent that the Committee's strongest supporters were the science agencies because of their concern for the supply and use of high-talent manpower, the Civil Service Commission because of its interest in internal manpower management, and the Bureau of the Budget, which sought help in the task of coordination. The agencies operating manpower programs, including the Labor Department, were unwilling to give up autonomy to anyone.

As long as the PCOM pursued the less sensitive aspects of its Title I jurisdiction—bringing about improvements in the techniques used by operating agencies to project their own manpower requirements and impacts and by statistical agencies to project national manpower requirements, or developing methodologies for projecting the manpower impacts of technological change—its existence created no problems. However, when it was suggested in late 1964 that the PCOM develop proposals for a "manpower program for the Great Society," it was made forcefully clear that no Cabinet member with manpower responsibilities would entrust his innovative ideas to an inter-agency committee.

The PCOM had a brief day in the sun in 1966. Congressional criticisms of overlap and confusion in the administration of manpower programs were loud, but a proposal to utilize the PCOM forestalled attempts to legislate program coordination. Three-man teams representing Labor, HEW, and OEO and operating under the aegis of the PCOM were assigned to major cities to facilitate coordination at the local level among federally supported manpower programs. Despite the difficulties of the task and the Committee's lack of real authority, progress was made during the few months of the effort. However, by early 1967 the pressures for coordination declined as unrest in the central city ghettoes became the center of attention. Overnight the three-man PCOM teams became the representatives of the Manpower Administration in launching the Concentrated Employment Program, an effort to focus the activities of all manpower programs on the slums of a few selected cities. Meanwhile, the other inter-agency functions had atrophied, and the activities of the statistically oriented PCOM subcommittees had ground to a halt for lack of attention. The President's Committee on Manpower had apparently been relegated to the crowded graveyard of inter-agency coordinating committees.

MANPOWER REPORT OF THE PRESIDENT

The annual *Manpower Report of the President* and the accompanying report of the Secretary of Labor were to be important factors in raising the level of interest in manpower issues. However, though conceived as an equal companion to the *Economic Report of the President*, it has not approached that degree of prestige. It lacks the *Economic Report*'s familiarity to the public gained by twenty years of publication. However, its policy impact is unlikely ever to be as great. The position of the Council of Economic Advisers as an integral part of the Executive Office of the President gives its report a greater air of authority. The *Economic Report* encompasses the entire range of national economic affairs, of which manpower considerations, even broadly defined, are only a part. The Council is not identified with a single operating department, nor is it burdened with the defense of particular programs. It has a broad area of subject matter from which to select and can report unsatisfactory conditions impersonally while taking credit for more favorable ones. The *Manpower Report*, on the other hand, bears some of the burdens of a house organ. It can be critical of the programs of neither the Labor Department or of other agencies with manpower responsibilities. There are pressures on its compilers to seek subjects which are inter- and intra-departmentally "safe." On general economic subjects it shares the tendency of most government reports to be descriptive rather than analytical.

Despite these almost inevitable constraints, the *Manpower Report* is widely distributed and quoted and has increased academic awareness of manpower problems. Some 30,000 copies are distributed annually, mostly in government and academic circles. The first two reports were primarily descriptive, but subsequent issues have become increasingly policy-oriented. The first aimed to increase awareness of the changing nature of the supply of and demand for labor, and the second to document the plight of various competitively disadvantaged groups in the labor market. The 1965 *Report* stressed the relationships between the various labor market and educational institutions and offered some descriptions of manpower programs. The 1966 *Report* took a modest step toward enunciating emerging manpower policies, and the 1967 *Report* presented a Labor Department appraisal of the contributions of various manpower programs. There have also been notable statistical contributions, such as the 1964 survey of the methods by which noncollege-trained workers obtained their skills, the 1966 projections of manpower requirements through 1970, and the 1967 survey of employment conditions in representative slums and depressed rural areas and the introduction of the "subemployment" concept.

The Senate Subcommittee on Employment and Manpower and the House Select Subcommittee on Labor attempted to increase the *Report*'s visibility and prestige by holding joint hearings on it[4] analogous to those held by the Joint Economic Committee on the *Economic Report*. However, the pressure of legislative business, the declining interest of the members of the subcommittees, and turnover of personnel limited to a single occurrence what was intended to become a tradition.

The act originally directed both the Secretary of Labor and

[4] *Manpower Report of the President*, 89th Cong., 1st sess., April 27–30, 1965.

of HEW to submit annual reports on training activities. In 1966 the former was relieved of his responsibility, on the assumption that his information would be included in the annual *Manpower Report*. While the 1967 *Manpower Report* contained MDTA's policy goals, statistical reporting was limited and analysis nonexistent. Apparently, the Department was too dissatisfied with the quality of its statistical data to dignify them by publication in an official document.

The *Manpower Report*'s contributions to manpower policy in the United States have been modest but significant. Although it does not make policy, it does raise issues and suggest the directions that public and private activity should take. It has undoubtedly increased public awareness and understanding of manpower problems.

MDTA RESEARCH PROGRAM

The research program under MDTA has been characterized by its small budget, its comparative insulation from political pressures, and the consistency with which its funds have been used to pursue the Act's remedial purposes. In contrast to the Vocational Education Act of 1963, which allocated 10 percent of all funds to research, the MDTA research budget exceeded 1 percent of the total only in the second fiscal year of operation. The funds for contract research in direct support of Title II training have remained at the second-year level and now represent less than ½ of 1 percent of the total MDTA budget. The additional funds for 1966 and after were for a grant program of a different nature.

The language of the research provisions of MDTA was drawn from the Administration bill. It reflects the recognition by administrators and technicians, most of them from the Bureau of Labor Statistics, that the new program would encounter a relatively uncharted field where an expanding base of knowledge would be important. Their direct concern with program support is apparent in the language of the Act which still stands. This legislative directive, in effect written by the Department to itself, did not establish a general program of manpower research: it ordered (1) evaluation of the impact of technological and related changes, establishment of techniques for their detection in advance, and development to solutions to the problems of displacement; (2) study of labor-mobility-restricting practices of employers and unions; (3) appraisal of "the adequacy of the nation's manpower development efforts to meet foreseeable manpower needs and recommendation of needed adjustment"; and (4) dissemination of the information thus obtained. In 1962 Congress showed little interest in any of the provisions of Title I, including the research provisions in general. Yet the program has been continually supported—though not expanded—by the appropriations committees, and there was no difficulty in obtaining grant authority and funds when they were requested.

The first year of the research program was a hectic one simply because the Act's first year was hectic. Without appropriations from March until September, the Labor Department was attempting to establish an administrative structure using the funds and staffs of existing programs. While USES personnel held regional meetings to familiarize state employment service personnel with the new Act's potential, a staff of four in OMAT were trying to promote general interest in the Act (without a budget it attracted little attention) to advise state agencies and other institutions on the establishment of training programs, and to develop a sound research program.

Development of a research program involved selecting areas for investigation and attracting competent researchers from other fields where funds were more readily available. Despite the lateness of its appropriations, the new agency faced the inevitable pressure to fund projects for a quick return in order to impress the congressional appropriations committees the following spring. Therefore, it was to the credit of the staff that the first year's contracts were with researchers, private organizations, and government statistical agencies of recognized competence, and only one contract was completed prior to the end of 1963 fiscal year.[5]

Each project was within research categories prescribed in the Act. Emphases were on foreseeing the impact of technological change, geographical and occupational labor mobility, accumulation of information on relevant European experience, development of methodology for measuring and projecting manpower requirements, and follow-up and evaluation of training projects. Not all of the projects turned out to be important contributions, but most, when completed, produced sound and significant results. This pattern of cautious planning and resistance to the inevitable political pressure appear typical of MDT's subsequent history.

In later years the range of research topics broadened. As policy emphasis shifted, research interest moved with it and sometimes ahead of it. As time passed, support was made available to less well known researchers, in part to broaden the base of manpower research interest and competence. An in-house research program was launched with a perspective wider than the responsibility for preparation of the annual *Manpower Report*. As examples, one in-house study had a significant impact on the 1965 Immigration Act, and another was among the first to call attention to the problem of the census undercount of Negro males.[6]

Little purpose would be served by listing and discussing the

[5] U.S., Department of Labor, Manpower Administration, Office of Manpower, Automation, and Training, *Manpower and Automation Research Sponsored by the Office of Manpower, Automation, and Training, July 1, 1962–June 30, 1963* (Washington, D.C.: U.S. Government Printing Office, 1963).

[6] U.S., Department of Labor, Manpower Administration, *Manpower and Immigration*, Manpower Report no. 4, rev. ed. (Washington, D.C.: U.S. Government Printing Office, 1965); *Unused Manpower: The Nation's Loss*, Manpower Research Bulletin no. 10 (Washington, D.C.: U.S. Government Printing Office, 1966).

research topics. A complete inventory and description is readily available.[7] Throughout its history, administrators of the research program have chosen to tie research to current and foreseeable policy issues as a service to policymakers and program operators rather than to pursue knowledge for its own sake. The policy orientation tends to be preserved by the fact that the Office of Manpower Research staff makes its own advance judgments of the key policy issues and solicits proposals for needed research, as well as funding *ad hoc* research proposals from applicants. Perhaps two-thirds of the contract budget is spent for research undertaken at the initiative of the OMR on topics of interest to the Manpower Administrator. In addition to determining and contracting for needed research, the policy orientation requires retention of sufficient funds for "crash" projects in case of crises demanding immediate attention. However, a few long-term, high-risk projects have been undertaken, including two independent studies by a university and a private research organization of the potential application of systems analysis to manpower adjustment and an in-house psychological study of the "meaning of work."

In 1965 Congress granted a request for authority and additional funds for institutional and individual research grants. The grants were to expand research capability by attracting competent graduate students, to encourage innovative research by more mature scholars, and to involve smaller colleges and universities in manpower research. In fiscal 1967 seven universities were awarded three-year institutional grants averaging $75,000 annually to launch long-range manpower research programs and to attract and develop research manpower. In addition, over one hundred small grants averaging about

[7] U.S., Department of Labor, Manpower Administration, *Manpower Research Projects, Sponsored by the U.S. Department of Labor Manpower Administration through June 30, 1967* (Washington, D.C.: U.S. Government Printing Office, 1967).

$10,000 each were made during 1966 and 1967, two-thirds of them to graduate students for dissertation research.

As the research program developed it became clear that funding and providing technical assistance were only a beginning for a program which placed priority on affecting policy, and growing emphasis was given to disseminating research results. A substantial publication program and the *Manpower Report* have been used to "spread the word," but a great deal of research has never and perhaps should never come to the attention of policy-makers. More recently, conferences have been organized around the results of specific projects, but these also seem more likely to inform other researchers than to influence makers of policy.

Evaluation of the research program is difficult. Where research has led directly and immediately to policy changes, the payoff is relatively clear. One research project demonstrating the need for basic education and higher training allowances was a major factor in the 1963 amendments to MDTA. Another project on the influence of pre-release skill training on recidivism led to the 1966 authorization for training in prison. Still another project identified the plight of Selective Service rejectees and led to a remedial program of employment and health assistance for them.[8]

Publications are another solid measure of research success, but their influence is difficult to assess. Eight books have been published commercially, in addition to a lengthy list of articles and government publications. The latest book, *The Negro and Apprenticeship*,[9] had a major impact on government policies and the practices of unions and employers even before its publication. Other contributions are less immediate and apparent. The commitment of a substantial number of young researchers of great promise, many of whom might

[8] The President's Task Force on Manpower Conservation, *One-Third of a Nation* (Washington, D.C.: U.S. Government Printing Office, 1964).
[9] Marshall and Briggs, *The Negro and Apprenticeship*.

have been attracted to alternative fields, is a clear long-range contribution to the manpower field.

Since the contributions of the research program cannot be measured and compared to its costs, the observer must depend upon his judgment. The research budget has been small. Through deliberation in constructing the research program, forethought in soliciting proposals, and selectivity in funding them, the funds have been carefully spent. This forethought includes recognition of the importance of building institutions and attracting competent scholars. Throughout the formulation and administration of the research program, the staff has profited from the advice and collaboration of the Subcommittee on Research of the National Manpower Advisory Committee. Various observers might disagree on areas of emphasis, topics funded, and degree of policy attachment, but those are largely matters of individual preference. The administrators of the program have understood the meaning of good research and pursued it.

EXPERIMENTATION AND DEMONSTRATION PROGRAM

The MDTA Experimentation and Demonstration program was created by Labor Department administrators rather than by Congress, but it has won legislative endorsement and has become a permanent feature of MDT. The term "experimentation and demonstration" was not descriptive of the Department's initial activities, and only recently have these functions become the primary objective. However, the program also continues to serve its original functions of providing (1) a source of flexible funds, unfettered by the rules and institutional constraints of the basic MDT program; and (2) a mechanism for offering technical assistance and financial motivation to public and private organizations willing to become more deeply involved in helping the disadvantaged.

E & D began as a reaction to the "creaming" proclivities of the early MDT efforts and as a way to circumvent distrusted "establishment" institutions. Until 1964 MDTA was the only significant source of federal assistance to those losing out in competition for the inadequate supply of jobs. With more experienced workers than they had funds or facilities to train, many state employment services and vocational educators were rejecting the undereducated as untrainable and older workers as unemployable and were interpreting "reasonable expectation of employment" to mean that training the seriously disadvantaged would be illegal.

Among the early OMAT staff members were a number of aggressive young reformers of the type who were later attracted to the Office of Economic Opportunity. They were placed in charge of a program of special projects which largely bypassed the state. employment services and the vocational schools. The legislative justification was derived from a liberal reading of the Title I authorization to "appraise the adequacy of the Nation's manpower development efforts to meet foreseeable manpower needs and recommend needed adjustments, including methods for promoting the most effective occupational utilization of and providing useful work experience and training opportunities for untrained and inexperienced youth."

OMAT and ARA funds were used in cooperation with the Office of Education and the Harvard University Language Institute to facilitate training Spanish-speaking and other undereducated migrants as farm equipment operators. Community-based organizations such as Community Progress, Inc. (New Haven, Connecticut), and Mobilization for Youth (New York City), which had been dependent on the Juvenile Delinquency and Youth Offenses Control Act and private foundations, now had a supplemental source of funds. Private nonprofit institutions like the YMCA, the Jewish Education and Vocational Service, and smaller single-unit institutions were able to broaden their horizons, formerly limited by their budgets, and take on the new role of serving the disadvantaged. Operations such as the Arizona Migrant and Indian Ministry, which served population groups in whom state-affiliated agencies had taken little interest, were underwritten. Funds were made available to meet emergency situations such as the Studebaker plant closing in South Bend Indiana, and to provide a flexibility not found in the ongoing training programs.

Although exciting, these developments were not welcomed by the state agencies, HEW, or the established bureaus of the Labor Department. The opposition reflected both the internal Labor Department issues already described and clashes of personality and philosophy. In addition to antipathy among agency heads, the irreverent E & D staff had little respect for orderly administrative procedures. Since the special projects concept was new to the Labor Department and there were no ready-made contracting procedures and fiscal standards, some administrators feared abuses by local contractors which would subject the Department to congressional criticism. They attempted to restrain the brash insurgents by their control of financial and personnel procedures. The opposition outside of the Labor Department was less personal but equally strong. E & D projects were financed by Title II funds that federal and state employment service and vocational education personnel were convinced they could use more effectively than the E & D sponsors.

In the long run orderly procedures won over productive chaos. When the state employment services and vocational educators took the issue to Congress, the House Education and Labor Committee concluded: "The more encouraging findings of the Committee relate to . . . these [special or demonstration] projects. . . . That these have been successful was abundantly demonstrated . . . the committee was impressed with the inventiveness, the scope and the promise evident in these projects. Since increased knowledge and experience is our most critical need . . . the Committee urges that . . . these special projects be continued and, if possible, expanded."[10] Later, Congress put money behind its endorsement by transferring the E & D efforts to Title I, thus ending the conflict for Title II funds. Though the E & D program was preserved, its "free-wheeling" days were ended. The program retained its flexibility but was tamed into an orderly and accepted operation of the Manpower Administration.

Though chaotic, the formative period was a productive one. Vital lessons were learned which contributed directly to the design of the antipoverty program in 1964. Some important innovations originated under MDTA sponsorship in those years. Often, projects already under way with foundation sponsorship or plans developed under small grants from the Juvenile Delinquency and Youth Offenses Control Act obtained their first substantial and dependable federal support from E & D funds. E & D emphasis was on spending money to help people rather than on experimentation to learn lessons. Nevertheless, the limited budget could not begin to meet the need for services. The fact of federal involvement brought to the federal agencies new awareness of the needs of disadvantaged members of society and familiarity with techniques for attacking their problems.

Despite a major change in management in 1965, the reorientation of the E & D program was evolutionary, not a sharp break with the past. Changes had begun earlier, when many of the more anti-establishment E & D personnel left for the Office of Economic Opportunity, the new frontier for serving the poor. The Economic Opportunity Act also provided an alternative and larger source of funds for local projects previously dependent upon MDTA funds. Problems arising

[10] U.S., Congress, House, Committee on Education and Labor, *Report To Accompany H.R. 8720*, p. 20.

from loose administrative procedures were already beginning to confront administrators. Audits were putting unfamiliar pressures on some local sponsors. Closing out projects produced more administrative problems than funding them. Demands were rising for proof of results. Yet existing projects had acquired considerable momentum, and the new administrative team was also interested in serving people as well as discovering and demonstrating new techniques.

Under the new management, funding continued for local projects, most of whose sponsors still considered their primary goal to be services for people in need. However, the E & D staff had become aware that to get any significant mileage from their limited funds something more than service had to be provided. Since proposed projects exceeded their budgetary capacity, they could pick those which served longer-run purposes, including experiments and demonstrations, though service was still the immediate goal of the sponsor. The project orientation changed slowly. Though disadvantaged groups remained the primary target, projects were chosen with a limited number of broad objectives in mind. The emphasis of the first three years of E & D shifted from providing jobs for youths to seeking solutions to the employment problems of slums and depressed rural areas. About one-third of E & D funds was still allocated to continuation of youth projects in fiscal 1967, but new programs appeared to be few and their proportion of the total was declining. New E & D youth programs appeared to be limited to providing summer employment and residential programs as alternatives to the Job Corps for youths whose enviroment was considered detrimental to effective rehabilitation. Funding has increased for programs for older workers, whose continuing under-representation in the regular MDTA program remains a serious problem. Projects were undertaken with the mentally retarded and the physically handicapped but were criticized for trespassing on the territory of vocational rehabilitation.

However, new projects emphasize minority group self-help, involvement of private employers in employing the disadvantaged, and attracting existing agencies to a number of newly recognized problem areas. MDTA-E & D has provided support for the Opportunities Industrialization Center in Philadelphia and, with OEO and the Ford Foundation, has helped spread the Philadelphia concept in several other cities. Operation SER, organizing self-help activities among Mexican-Americans in the Southwest, and Project Pride in Washington, D.C., a voluntary organization employing Negro youth in rat-killing and cleanup activities, could also be included in the self-help category.

An example of the involvement of private employers in such projects is Jobs Now in Chicago, which has become the prototype for one component of the concentrated employment program. It recruits young gang members, puts them through a two-week orientation period stressing work attitudes and appearance, places them with cooperating employers, and provides job coaches for both the boys and their supervisors to help them hold their new jobs. Other projects focus on especially stubborn employment problems such as the matter of transportation of workers from ghettoes to suburban jobs.

The bonding demonstration project merits attention, particularly because it has a unique result. Congress singled it out for specific sanction. Protection was purchased from a commercial firm for employers who refused to hire workers with police records unless bonded. In the initial stages over 200 persons were bonded and placed in seven locations, with only three defaults. When informed that bonding was available, most employers re-examined their hiring practices and hired the worker, either without bond or through their own established bonding arrangements. Others were forced to admit that the bond was an excuse to avoid hiring persons with arrest records.

This transition from a service to a problem orientation now appears to be entering a new phase. E & D administrators have begun organizing their projects into a three-part program consisting of institution-building, probing for new activities to be performed by existing public agencies, and building a more formal experimentation and demonstration effort around a concept of experimental manpower laboratories.

The primary objective of the first part of the program is the development of nongovernmental institutions involving, as well as serving, the disadvantaged. The intent of the second part is the examination of the activities of public agencies, identification of needed services not currently provided, and underwriting of efforts to fill the gaps. The hope is that agency goals and orientation can be changed sufficiently to make the services permanent. Each of these objectives provides a rationale for a choice among various proposals and is designed to get a bigger payoff from projects not greatly different from those which have been supported in the past.

The third objective involves a major departure from E & D procedure and, for the first time, involves formal experimentation and demonstration. Experimental laboratories or a combination of operational experience and analytical competence will provide data to measure the success or failure of concepts and techniques rather than the administrative capability of project sponsors. The first such laboratory links Mobilization for Youth (MFY) in New York City, an experienced sponsor of NYC, MDT-OJT, and other manpower and antipoverty programs, with the Columbia University School of Social Work. Plans call for linking a mental hospital with a university in one location and a prison system with a research foundation in another. Only a few such laboratories with substantial funding—$750,000 per year in the MFY-Columbia case—are contemplated. The hope is that experience, continuity, high caliber personnel, and rigorous methodology can be combined in experiments of sufficient size to provide the visibility needed for demonstration.

While the contributions of the MDTA-E & D program cannot be measured, many techniques for the delivery of manpower services to the disadvantaged in the past few years have been developed or refined in E & D-sponsored programs. Their lessons have been incorporated into legislation, and service-rendering agencies have adopted new practices and modified old ones. Whether the institutions to serve the disadvantaged will be created remains an open question. The experimental laboratory is an attractive concept but must be tested by experience.

In choosing among project proposals, the E & D administrators have deliberately maintained *ad hoc* consideration of proposals rather than, for instance, establishing fixed guidelines or appointing professional review panels to pass on project proposals. Because of the freedom with which funds can be used and the involvement with projects which furnish services, the program has come under substantial political pressure. Although very few projects without merit are funded for political reasons, political considerations have been important in many, including some of the most productive ones. Since there is usually freedom to improve project proposals for which funding is assured, administrators do not consider the political pressures too great in return for the direct contact with the "real world" of employment.

More difficult than avoiding unpromising projects is resisting the premature enthusiasms of success. The Opportunities Industrialization Centers and Jobs Now projects, supported by E & D, were successful in the environments within which they developed and attracted enthusiasm in the continued quest for answers to difficult employment problems. There has thus been reason to question their transference to other environments without adequate identification of the reasons for their initial success.[11] A program not protected by layers of manuals, direc-

[11] See "Transferability of Manpower Programs," in *Examination of the War on Poverty, Staff and Consultant Reports,* prepared for the Senate Committee on Labor and Public Welfare Subcommi*.ee on Employment, Manpower and Poverty by Arnold Nemore, vol. 2.

tives, program letters, and allocations has no defense against these threats, but flexibility appears to have been worth the risk.

The overall federal government involvement in demonstration programs has been justly criticized as a device for appearing to serve needs while refusing to allocate meaningful sums of money.[12] For an individual program, however, it makes sense to have a relatively unfettered fund for developing new techniques, building new institutions, and providing leverage for reorientation of old ones.

Unfortunately, Congress, which praised and expanded E & D from 1963 to 1966, cut its funds back sharply in 1967 and refused to expand it for 1968. The reason given was that, with four or five years' experience, experimentation was no longer a pressing necessity. More cynical observers have suggested that the minority group emphases led some congressional appropriations committee members to consider the E & D budget expendable "nigger money." Whatever the reason, the disenchantment is unfortunate. With economic and social conditions constantly changing, some aspect of the program should always be forging ahead of the regular training effort. In addition, E & D has come to serve not just the Title II program but the total effort of the Manpower Administration.

The E & D program remains in many ways a flexible source of funds to be used for special projects no other program is authorized or willing to undertake. It may serve persons ineligible for other programs. It may underwrite activities either too speculative for other programs or not within the purview of the well-defined ones. It may serve groups which local mores or political structures will not allow established institutions to serve. E & D funds may also be used to fund projects which catch the attention of the Secretary of Labor, the Presi-

[12] Martin Rein and S. M. Miller, "Social Action on the Installment Plan," *Transaction*, January–February, 1967, pp. 31–38.

dent, or a key member of Congress. Nevertheless, there appears to be a substantial change from the earlier period of a primarily *ad hoc* service orientation. With proposals far in excess of budgets, establishment of priorities is necessary, and as long as the administrators have in mind a framework for selection, a rational policy can be pursued.

As a result of inadequate staffing, most E & D projects have not received adequate supervision or technical assistance from the Labor Department. Identification and evaluation of E & D experience is necessary. Dissemination of project results in such a way that operating programs profit is a continuing challenge. The program objectives are now more clearly defined. There have been significant demonstration effects though still little formal experimentation. The E & D program is difficult to evaluate because experiments are expected to fail, and successes are rarely clear-cut. The critical evaluator is only pitting his judgment against that of the administrator that the projects rejected had more potential than those funded. In general, one can only register a judgment that the money has been reasonably spent on projects making a useful contribution in terms of the knowledge disseminated, the institutions developed, and the people served. The most reassuring factor is that the administrators of the E & D program appear to know what they want to accomplish—the first necessary step toward getting it done.

LABOR MOBILITY DEMONSTRATION PROJECTS

The labor mobility demonstration projects authorized under MDTA deserve to be discussed individually because in the United States they offered the first opportunity to test the effectiveness of a general program of relocation assistance in reducing unemployment. European experience had suggested adding relocation to our kit of manpower tools, but policies forbade it. Relocation experience in this country had been limited to special circumstances and special groups, such as American Indians and Cuban refugees or the Armour Automation Fund activities, and they have been too few to use as a basis for generalization.[13]

In 1963 the amendments to MDTA, although providing no additional funds for relocation, allowed the Secretary of Labor to use up to $4 million of Title II appropriations for that purpose. The 1965 amendments transferred the program to Title I and authorized an appropriation of $5 million per year. Relocation projects were not undertaken until fiscal 1965, but they have continued in subsequent years. The time problems in follow-up, reporting, and analysis are such that detailed results are currently available only for the 1965 program. However, an examination of individual project reports for fiscal years 1966 and 1967 suggests that they will not differ appreciably from 1965.

The legal constraints imposed upon the mobility projects were deliberate. Only unemployed or underemployed persons for whom there was no reasonable expectation of employment in their own communities were eligible. A bona fide job offer was also required prior to relocation. Administrative guidelines added the requirement that the job be one which otherwise would not be filled by qualified local workers, by local workers who could be trained, or by relocation of nearby workers. Though grants up to 50 percent or loans up to 100 percent of relocation expenses were authorized, the prevailing pattern has been to combine 50 percent grants with 50 percent loans.

In fiscal 1965 eleven projects were conducted by state employment services, three by universities, and two by private nonprofit institutions, one institution specializing in the problems of older workers and the other serving a depressed rural area. Most sponsors were more interested in relocating people

[13] George P. Shultz and Arnold R. Weber, *Strategies for the Displaced Worker* (New York: Harper & Row, Inc., 1967).

than in testing the results of the relocation. No project utilized a control group for comparison and data on both pre- and postrelocation employment, and information on earning experience was limited. On the other hand, the circumstances were sufficiently different from project to project to offer numerous insights into the problems and potentials of relocation.

Two projects involved unemployed MDTA graduates. Two others served technical and skilled workers laid off by defense contract cancellations. Four recruited workers from depressed coal mining areas, and three drew from other depressed rural areas. All but the defense plant projects and a project serving workers displaced by the closing of the Studebaker plant in South Bend, Indiana, involved rural to urban shifts to some extent. One was limited to older workers, another to youths; two worked with technologically displaced farm workers. Some projects served homogeneous groups of workers laid off by a particular employment crisis; others drew applicants at random from active state employment service files; and a few undertook intensive outreach efforts among isolated rural residents.

Despite authorization to spend up to $4 million, the 1965 program had a total expenditure of little more than $1 million. Of 14,000 workers who were screened, 6,200 met the eligibility requirements. Two-thirds of those eligible expressed interest in moving, but only 1,300 relocated. Since all could not be offered jobs, it is uncertain how many preferred not to relocate and how many did not have the opportunity to do so. Follow-up was limited to two and in some cases four months after relocation. Within that time, 20 percent had returned home and another 20 percent had changed jobs. Of those who remained, over 80 percent liked their new neighborhoods and were satisfied with their move. Most relocations were within a state, but a substantial minority were interstate—one project moved aircraft workers from New York to California. The Labor Department claims a highly favorable benefit-cost ratio for the program, but earnings estimates both before and after relocation were based on assumptions which, though not unreasonable, were supported only by the hourly wage rate of the job held after relocation. The employment and earnings which would have occurred in the absence of relocation and the extent of unemployment over time after relocation are not known.

The first-year projects were a productive learning experience. Relocation allowances were less than expected, averaging under $300 with the average by project ranging from $100 to $800. (Table 5–2). The costs were lower than anticipated because few workers had household effects worth moving, moves were shorter, and dependents were fewer. About half the cost represented lump-sum living allowances to support the family until the first pay check; 30 percent represented transportation and storage of household goods; and 20 percent represented travel allowances. The cost of administering the program was double the total allowance cost. Administrative costs varied widely by project and depended upon difficulties in recruiting and the need for counseling and various other supportive services. Various start-up costs, the inevitable false starts, and unproductive experimentation make it doubtful that the cost ratios of the first year will hold for subsequent years.

The experience with repayment of loans was very discouraging. Ten months after completion of the projects, 55 percent of the loans were delinquent. Neither the state employment services nor the private sponsors had the experience or the inclination to act as collection agencies. There was also reluctance to press those who had returned home or were struggling with high living costs in their new locations. There was some initial difficulty with potential relocatees who accepted the moving allowances and then failed to move. This was solved by parceling out reimbursements as expenses occurred and by paying part of the living allowances before and part after the move

Table 5-2

Costs and Results of 1965 Mobility Projects

State or Contractor	No. Relocated	Percent Remaining	Cost per Relocation	Cost per "Permanent" Relocation	Allowance						Administrative Costs	Estimated Hourly Wage (available projects)	Origin, Destination, and Characteristics of Relocatees
					Total Allowances[a]	Living Allowance	Transportation Of persons	Transportation Of goods[b]	Grants	Loans			
					State Employment Service Projects								
West Virginia	75	53	$ 499	$ 935	$162	$123	$ 26	$ 12	$ 81	$ 81	$339	$2.00	Rural and coal miners to interstate urban
Virginia	200	64	443	686	212	145	25	41	106	105	274	1.88	Rural and coal miners to intrastate urban
Utah	43	88	1,083	1,225	634	236	78	320	318	313	478	2.57	Missile workers, interstate
New York	177	93	943	1,018	807	125	252	430	403	403	350	2.72	Aircraft workers, interstate
Montana	20	80	517	647	246	177	19	50	123	123	321	2.14	Seasonally unemployed, mining to intrastate urban
Missouri	21	71	517	n.a.	312	240	38	24	123	180	n.a.	n.a.	Farm workers, rural to rural intrastate
Minnesota	25	80	n.a.	n.a.	279	177	29	72	155	124	n.a.	n.a.	Youths, rural and mining, to intra- and interstate urban
Kentucky	24	79	n.a.	n.a.	165	108	29	27	165	—	n.a.	n.a.	Rural and coal miners to intrastate urban
Illinois	95	74	575	780	256	169	30	56	129	127	319	2.04	Rural and coal miners to urban intrastate
California	25	100	n.a.	n.a.	429	183	49	195	199	228	n.a.	n.a.	Employment service job applicants, urban to urban intrastate

Private Contractors' Projects

Tuskegee Institute	103	69	957	1,388	279	192	49	37	144	135	678	2.04	Rural Negroes to urban intrastate and interstate
Southern Illinois University	125	60	640	1,060	268	182	28	58	142	126	372	n.a.	Rural and coal miners, interstate
Northern Michigan University	108	89	776	873	286	186	49	51		286	562	2.09	Rural miners and lumbermen to urban intra- and interstate
North Carolina Fund	293	97	475	492	114	104	3	7	73	41	367	1.46	Whites, Negroes, and Indians, rural to urban interstate
National Council on Aging	2	100	n.a.	n.a.	72	—	6	—	72	—	n.a.	n.a.	Older workers, urban to urban intrastate
Total, All Projects	1,336	80	651	821	292	150	52	90	143	149	391	2.10	

a Includes averages for those receiving allowances only; 140 trainees received no financial assistance.
b Includes storage.

was completed. The experience strongly argued for reliance on grants rather than loans, both for economy of administration and to prevent overburdening people already under heavy financial handicaps.

A variety of factors were involved in failures to relocate or to stay in the new location. The relocatees were almost all male, and their mobility was highly correlated with age. Of all relocatees 70 percent were white, but an even higher percentage of eligible Negroes were relocatees. MDTA graduates and those with many dependents were most willing to move. Education appeared to make little difference, although skilled technical workers had a higher propensity to relocate and were most likely to stay with their new jobs. Unskilled workers found it difficult to obtain jobs and to take advantage of the program. When relocation was combined with basic education and skill training, willingness to move was higher and the return rate lower.

The project sponsors met considerable local opposition from supply areas. In rural areas growers were often hostile to relocation of their potential labor supply. In industrial areas some companies refused to supply the names of workers on layoff. Resistance was particularly strong when attempts were made to relocate younger workers and those with skills, experience, or education. Other opposition came from politicians, civil rights workers, and community action agencies. The state employment service sponsors proved most vulnerable to the local opposition because of their local and state governmental connections.

Eligibility for unemployment insurance and availability of public assistance were factors discouraging relocation. The slightest improvement or promise of improvement in the local employment outlook, even though only temporary or seasonal, was often enough to change the minds of potential relocatees. Occasionally, changes in local conditions during the course of a project simply removed the reasons for relocation.

Selection of relocation areas sometimes ruled out potential relocatees. In some cases, members of minority groups were not moved for fear they would not be accepted in the new area. Housing, particularly for minority group members and large families, was a serious obstacle, as were high costs of living and lack of health and other social services. A pervasive problem for the unskilled was the lack of job opportunities.

The decision to return home from the relocation area was primarily based on such noneconomic factors as ties of kinship, climate, school systems, and general living conditions. Nonmonetary supportive services, such as counseling and preparation for the move, help with moving arrangements, and assistance in finding housing in the new area, in keeping the new job, and in resolving family adjustment problems, were crucial in retaining in the program those with the least travel experience and knowledge of urban life.

The state employment services demonstrated their ability to identify large numbers of relocatees, test and screen them, and refer them to employment service offices in the receiving cities. In all, the employment agencies of twenty-eight states were involved. Their ability to handle outreach among the disadvantaged was not tested because they had an ample supply of eligible workers in their applicant files. However, the regular interarea placement procedures proved too slow and cumbersome, and direct telephone and personal contacts between offices in supply and in demand areas was necessary. The private institutions were involved in the more difficult and unusual situations, but they tended to be specialists in dealing with particular groups in narrowly restricted geographical areas. One private contractor attained an impressive success rate in moving poor whites, Negroes, and Indians from a rural depressed area. They were helped with the physical details of their moves, and when housing became a problem an apartment building was purchased and trailers were rented. Counseling was provided for homemaking as well as for work.

The project with the lowest return rate (3 percent) provided the greatest support, but it also involved a relatively limited move that made weekend visits home possible. Unfortunately, overall return rates were measured only during the first two to four months. Subsequently, this project has experienced a high rate of return. This may be true for others where short distances make mobility easy in either direction.

The residents of coal-mining areas, especially West Virginia and Kentucky, were the most reluctant to move and the least likely to remain in their new location. However, the more mobile workers had already left these depressed areas. It is interesting to note that an apparently high proportion of relocatees (the exact number is unknown) had either moved to another area once before and had returned or had worked away from home leaving their families behind.

The impression gained in most of the projects was that no significant number of workers would have moved at that time without financial assistance. The lack of money on which to live until the first pay check would have been a more serious obstacle than the actual expense of moving. Defense workers would probably have obtained less skilled jobs and remained where they were. Since there was so much outmigration from other areas, it is likely that the projects' major contribution was to affect the timing and destination of the moves. In determining unaided moves, kinship and ethnic patterns are more important than economic opportunity. The frequent result is increased concentrations of low-skilled workers in an area already oversupplied with them. By requiring a firm job offer, the mobility projects increased the economic rationality of the moves. Many of the demand areas showed remarkable ability to absorb low-skilled, though not "bottom-of-the-barrel," workers.

Where large numbers of workers were available, employers sent recruiters, but they were unwilling to do so where the numbers were few and the area isolated. Employer insistence on personal interviews and physical examinations in the latter case presented serious financial obstacles. Over and above the relocation allowances originally contemplated, in many cases, it also proved necessary to pay travel expenses for interviews. Only in one project were wives included on the advance trip but with favorable results.

Though no data are available to compare costs with benefits, the experiences in the 1965 mobility project appear to justify modest positive conclusions. The proportion of eligible workers wanting to move was small. Those whose need for relocating was greatest, on objective grounds, were the most reluctant to do so. The legal requirement that a bona fide job offer had to exist in advance of relocation increased the probability of success. However, the financial assistance offered by the project apparently encouraged mobility and was probably even more important in retention of the new job. The lump-sum living allowance eased the difficult time until receipt of the first pay check. As important as financial assistance was, the assurance of a job and guidance in surmounting the difficulties of moving and resettling were even more crucial. A strong case was made for combining basic education, skill training, and relocation.

The 1965 projects were limited by a one-year expiration date. Later projects were designed for more extensive follow-up and evaluation. Attempts were made to incorporate more specific research in the project design and to expand the range of questions explored. Most built on the 1965 projects, but several new ones were added. Additional outreach, social services, and placement techniques were tested. Relocatees include MDT graduates, migrant workers, Negroes, Mexican-American laborers, and welfare recipients, and various levels and combinations of relocation allowances are being tested.

The Travelers' Aid Society and the Smaller Communities Teams of the USES are being used. An interregional project involving twelve eastern states has been set up to test effectiveness of projects operating in a broader geographical setting and with more adequate staffing at the receiving end of the hiring transaction. Whereas the 1965 projects emphasized rural-to-urban shifts, some of the later ones experimented with slum-to-suburb relocation. The delay in reporting and evaluating the results of these projects is frustrating, but when the data are available for analysis, they should be enlightening.

By the summer of 1967, a total of 6,500 unemployed and underemployed workers had been relocated, and the projects were continuing to arrange 3,000 to 4,000 moves per year. There had been no appreciable change in cost over the first year. However, it was still hoped that a permanent program might develop greater economies in administrative costs.

The Labor Department, on the basis of the three years of relocation experience, requested a permanent budget for the program of nearly $15 million a year, expecting to relocate about 20,000 workers annually. Such a program offers no major solution to unemployment. The mobility of American workers is already high, and few more are likely to move because of this assistance or have skills in demand in other labor markets. However, those few should have the opportunity to do so. Combining relocation assistance with training may increase the number. Many geographically mobile workers make irrational moves, the rationalization of which would be a useful contribution. Results for 1966 and 1967 similar to those of 1965 would lend strong support to the Labor Department's conclusion that a permanent and large-scale mobility program is now justified.

6:

Continuing Issues

IT is clear that MDTA has represented a prudent investment of public funds. Opportunities for improving administrative effectiveness, training techniques, and the quality of services to trainees and employers are present in this as in any program. However, desirable objectives have been attained at modest costs. Four basic issues which have been debated throughout the program's history remain unresolved and encompass major policy decisions which will determine its future: (1) should the program emphasize upgrading the labor force or rehabilitating the disadvantaged; (2) what are the relative advantages of institutional training and OJT; and what should be the balance between them; (3) what should be the relative federal and state roles in policy and operation; and (4) is a permanent program needed and if so what should be its nature and size?

OBJECTIVES AND PRIORITIES

In line with national policy objectives which are less well accepted at local levels, the manpower development and training program has placed increasing emphasis on training and jobs for the disadvantaged. Many people at the national level and even more at the state and local levels complain that MDT is becoming "just another poverty program." They would be happier to see MDT concentrating on labor shortages and upgrading the labor force, serving the disadvantaged only as a part of the total operation. Their preferences are evident in legislation supporting fresher courses for professionals out of the labor force, part-time upgrading projects for the employed, and union-sponsored courses to upgrade workers with low skill levels.

The alternatives raise fundamental questions concerning the nature and purpose of the program. Its nature has been remedial: to train or retrain those beyond the reach of the education system who are already in or on the fringes of the labor market and who are having employment trouble. Its emphasis has been on the individual and his problems—first the displaced adult with a history of long-term employment, later the school dropout, and now the competitively disadvantaged —not the needs of the economy.

While facilitating the employment of the unemployed and upgrading the quality of the labor force are justifiable social goals, they raise two questions. The first is one of priorities. Training the disadvantaged upgrades the labor force, but the opposite is not necessarily true. Given the limited MDTA funds and the human and social costs and benefits involved, the goal of enabling the disadvantaged to share in the progress and prosperity of the economy would seem to merit priority. The second question is one of means rather than ends. Preparing workers for employment is one purpose of the educational system and is the specific objective of vocational education. Offerings of the latter include both secondary and post-secondary training and evening courses for employed adults.

Institutional MDT training is also a part of vocational education but with two differences. The first is that the MDT enrollee is in the labor market and is in immediate need of a job and income. The vocational education student is more often preparing to enter the labor force or is pursuing a longer-term goal of upgrading his skills. The symbol of this difference is the MDT allowance, received by five of every six trainees. Vocational education students are expected to be self-supporting, but MDT trainees either require allowances for support or, in the case of youthful school dropouts, for motivation. The proper comparison for OJT is with the vocational education cooperative programs, in which students spend part of their time in school and part on the job. For these students earnings are secondary to learning: for the OJT enrollees who are full-time labor force participants, income is the primary consideration.

The second difference between MDT and vocational education is the willingness and ability of the former program to serve those who have been too often ignored. Under MDT vocational educators have effectively served those with deficient educational preparation and have developed new remedial tools to do so. The 1963 Vocational Education Act directed vocational education to move in this direction but provided no incentive for action. By 1966 "persons who have academic, socio-economic or other handicaps that prevent them from succeeding in the regular vocational education program"— one of the major emphases of the 1963 Act—represented only 1 percent of all persons enrolled in vocational education programs. If vocational education can be moved to assume responsibility for such persons, MDT can and should be limited to remedial efforts on behalf of those already in the labor market who need special assistance.

Such a decision would help resolve troublesome issues concerning the content of training. Many critics of the MDT program, particularly vocational educators, have pointed out the narrowness and brevity of its courses and its focus on present rather than future demands. A related charge is that anxiety to ensure employment encourages training for low-skilled, low-paid, high-turnover jobs for which training is not required by job content, though it may be necessary in order to provide access to them for the trainees involved. The latter criticism, while often justified, is not a necessary result of training of immediate employment. Training should be for the best job available to the trainee, but the nature of the program requires that it lead directly to a job. In cases where only low-wage, dead-end jobs are available, a job creation program is needed, rather than a training program. The 1966 amendments made possible inclusion of basic education and other training to increase employability, but this additional training should also be directly oriented toward jobs.

Even agreement that MDT should continue as a remedial program does not determine the specific clientele on whom it should focus attention. The more disadvantaged the trainee, the greater the training expenditure, particularly since a heavy increment of basic education is required. Post-training earnings are likely to be lower and employment less favorable the more disadvantaged the trainee, limiting the program's demonstrable accomplishments. The choice may have political as well as economic and social consequences. MDTA's "honeymoon" with Congress has been in large part a product of its conservative stance. A program to assist responsible heads of families, deprived of their jobs and skills through no fault of their own by measures which can be demonstrated to pay for themselves from increased tax yields is likely to meet criticism only if most maladroitly administered. A program which undertakes the task of reaching the "left-outs" is less likely to achieve widespread political support.

The social costs of failure to narrow the division between the prosperous many and the disadvantaged few are becoming increasingly apparent, however. MDT has thus far not been a program for those who are alienated from society. It has been effective for those willing to learn and to work but lacking in skills and opportunity. Members of low-income families have apparently predominated, but probably only the most stable of these families have seen served. To a reasonable degree, the program has reached Negroes, youths with more than elementary but less than high school education, and the more employable poor. It has yet to involve in adequate numbers older workers, those with eight years or less of education, and the rural unemployed and underemployed, and it has failed to pentrate the ghetto to any substantial degree.

The under-representation in MDT of those with the least education stems from both deficiencies in teaching techniques and lack of employer acceptance. The under-representation of older workers is not readily explained but needs study. The neglect of rural areas results from the lack of training facilities, job opportunities, and effective rural employment services. Skill centers offer an approach to the problems of the ghetto but face problems of technique, image, and the immobility which often makes an almost impenetrable barrier of a few miles. Correction of these imbalances will be expensive and will result in fewer trainees per dollar. Jobs which would have otherwise been filled by the less disadvantaged may have to be re-allocated, but meeting the needs of the most disadvantaged has the highest priority and is worth the cost.

As MDTA administrators increase their emphasis on serving the disadvantaged, they should not be unduly disturbed by criticisms of "creaming." Given the pressures to demonstrate success, the relative accessibility or inaccessibility of various groups, and the natural human tendency to follow lines of least resistance, it is doubtful that any program can avoid the tendency to select the best qualified from among eligible clients. All that can be done is to set eligibility criteria so that the "cream" will be skimmed from the desired groups rather than from those more favorably situated. It is by no means obvious that the process of pushing over the dividing line between failure and success those for whom the distance between the two is shortest and the expense is least is undesirable.

If funds were unlimited, the logical approach would be to start at the head of the line and work back. It would only be necessary to make sure that public funds were not spent on those who would have achieved the same success without the support. It is the limited availability of resources and, therefore the need for priorities that dictates emphasis on the disadvantaged. Pronouncements in favor of balance rarely provide concrete policy guides. Manpower development and training efforts should stress enrollment of the disadvantaged and yet be satisfied to serve those who can reasonably hope to achieve employability, so that the expenditure per trainee will not soar so high that the number who can be served, will be unduly limited.

INSTITUTIONAL VS. ON-THE-JOB TRAINING

The second issue is a technical rather than a political one. What is the most efficient training method for specific individuals and for specific occupations? Institutional training offers a controlled situation for imparting knowledge in a consistent and coherent sequence selected by the instructor. It is best suited to broad concepts and general skills. However, institutional offerings have often been narrowly constructed to meet a particular employer's demands without his guarantee of a job after training. On-the-job-training provides a job and income during training and a greater likelihood of job retention after training. It does not require purchase of new equipment and reduces the problem of recruiting instructors. It provides the atmosphere and discipline of the work place, which cannot be duplicated in the classroom. Since the disadvantaged trainee often associates school with failure, he may find it easier to learn on the job.

However, the employer is more likely to hire the trainee on the basis of current rather than potential ability, and he is usually uninterested in providing training beyond what will fill his own immediate needs. Recruitment and training of employees are a normal cost of doing business. It is difficult to justify subsidizing employers' training costs unless they are rendering a social service. One such service is to employ and train those who otherwise would be rejected. Improving the quality of the labor force is also a social service but currently has lower priority than employing the disadvantaged. To subsidize training for those who would have been trained anyway, or to underwrite training no broader than that which the employer would have provided to meet his own needs, makes no net addition to the welfare of society.

Institutional training may also be no broader than what the employer would pay for, but it attempts to meet the needs of many employers, rather than those of a particular employer. It may be unfair to assume that the content of institutional training is broader than that of OJT but none the less OJT must demonstrate that its results are significantly different from what would have occurred in its absence. Considering the great pressure to fill slots and expand the OJT program during 1966 and 1967, it is not surprising that a less disadvantaged group was recruited in those years. However, greater care should now be taken to ensure that it is primarily the disadvantaged who are served. The argument for upgrading employed workers in order to open jobs for the disadvantaged is valid, but only if administrative machinery is set up to assure that the new jobs do in fact materialize.

Given the objectives of MDT, both institutional and on-the-job training have their advantages and disadvantages. Coupling is the logical approach, but administrative problems have made it difficult. Incorporating basic education into the work day as part of OJT is an alternative currently being tested. The selection of training methods should be based upon particular circumstances, but those making the decisions are not neutral. The issue has been determined by an arbitrary division of funds and authorizations at the national level.

Low per trainee cost and high post-training employment rates resulted in the decision to expand OJT. HEW officials argue that the decision left idle skill centers and other facilities which would have provided training of more lasting worth. The Manpower Administration's rebuttal is that within the limited budget the number of trainees can be expanded only by emphasizing the least-cost method. Yet the trend is toward higher OJT reimbursements in order to encourage employers to employ and train the disadvantaged.

The lack of BAT staff has prevented adequate monitoring of OJT projects. Despite the inherent difficulty of making sure that employers are reimbursed only for hiring and training those they would otherwise not have hired and that a significant amount of training results, a more serious attempt at evaluation, which could be made, has been neglected.

Only longitudinal studies over an extended period will determine the relative long-term advantages of the institutional, OJT, and coupled approaches. The choice between quantity and quality—if that proves to be the real choice—will remain a value judgment. Until the evidence is in, something like the current balance between the two training methods seems appropriate.

FEDERAL AND STATE ROLES IN PROGRAM ADMINISTRATION

The federal-state issue will simmer as long as MDT is considered an emergency program, but controversy will increase if it becomes permanent. MDTA falls squarely between the vocational education patterns in which federal grants almost totally unfettered by guidelines are made to the states, and the Economic Opportunity Act approach, which is to bypass states and often local governments in order to deal directly with a variety of *ad hoc* organizations on a contract basis. The initial state and local resistance to national decision-making has decreased with time. The use of state institutions as project-by-project contractors assures discussion, negotiation, and often compromise with state and local officials who have their own ideas and priorities. However, federal decisions prevail unless the opposition reaches the ears of key members of

Congress. The price often paid for this national decision-making and federal project-by-project review is ignoring differences among localities, heavy involvement of federal personnel in project administration, and difficulties in maintaining continuous use of local personnel and facilities.

Even with basic policy set at the federal level, programs vary from state to state. Trainees vary by race, educational level, and other demographic characteristics much more widely than can be explained by differences in populations. Costs vary from $670 per trainee in Connecticut to $1,920 per trainee in Wyoming, largely, but not entirely, because of differences in subsistence and allowance costs.

Post-training employment has varied from 38 percent in Delaware to 83 percent in South Dakota. No simple explanation such as level of economic activity or unemployment rate can account for these variations because some areas, such as Puerto Rico, with a high general level of unemployment had a low unemployment rate among MDT completers, and vice versa. Interest also varies: twenty-six states used less than their 1966 allocations, permitting re-allocation of funds to more aggressive states (Table 2–1).

Most federal officials argue for strong central control of policy, fearing that state and local officials may be too susceptible to political pressures. However, those same pressures can be applied by interested congressmen at the national level. Political influence has led federal officials to approve programs proposed by cronies or to continue a less than successful program because a president promised it in a regional speech following a superficial tour of an area.

Some Labor Department administrators see in vocational education "horrible examples" of what could happen to MDTA if the states were given too much discretion. They fail to give sufficient weight to the Smith-Hughes and George-Barden Act requirements that federal funds be spent within the specified categories, which, in the past, tied much of the vocational education effort to declining occupational sectors. However, some local vocational educators who objected to federal control most vociferously at first, now admit the tendency to perpetuate certain kinds of training regardless of need because of the existence of instructors, equipment, and courses. They agree that the MDTA project review process tends to increase responsiveness to labor market developments. However, they also argue that the tendency of projects to concentrate—to settle down to training for occupations in almost continuous demand—makes that flexibility less important.

The development of skill centers puts the issue in a new light. *Ad hoc* funding of projects with regular public or private schools might be resented by state and local educators, but they had little obligation to such projects. Establishment of institutions totally financed by MDTA implies continued support. Instructors have thus far been willing to work on an hourly basis without fringe benefits or tenure, but there appears to be an increasing desire among them for greater employment security. State vocational educators provided some security by funding projects for longer periods but with several groups of trainees. As previously noted, this device has now been halted by Bureau of the Budget and congressional pressure for appropriated funds to be spent in the current fiscal year. The failure to mesh the federal budgeting and congressional appropriating processes with the necessity for advance planning of each academic year is a serious obstacle to smooth federal-state relations in education. The MDT program had, in part, surmounted this obstacle by use of its authority to spend committed funds in the succeeding fiscal year. The real danger in revoking this authority and pressing the states for prompt current expenditures may be to "throw the baby out with the bath water."

Even with the multisectional approach, the out-of-phase appropriations process, as well as occasional delays in project review, still causes gaps in funding. Federal personnel have stayed abreast of the current work load but have done so at the expense of neglecting monitoring and evaluation activities. Expansion of the program would put further strain on this federal administrative capacity.

The OJT program has more complex dimensions. Since there is no state agency corresponding to BAT, state officials tend to prefer institutional training and resent federal directives fixing the relative institutional-OJT allocations. A number of states which use all their allotted institutional funds and more turn back unused OJT funds consistently. The national OJT contractors, though not bound by state lines, fund their training slots from state allocations but often do so without informing state agencies. All OJT national and community contracts, as well as others for more than $500,000, have been approved at the national level. To leave OJT promotion to state personnel might increase its acceptance by small intrastate firms but would probably limit it among the large interstate firms who control the most and often the best jobs.

The developing Cooperative Area Manpower Planning System (CAMPS) may ease federal-state problems. Through it, the federal agencies can establish guidelines and approve annual plans for areas, states, and regions. The states can then approve, and have funded automatically, individual projects within the state plan without the necessity of federal project-by-project approval. The federal agencies could complete the cycle by monitoring state operations to assure that the plans were followed and by evaluating performance as a basis for approval for future plans, all without the necessity of detailed administrative involvement in individual projects.

The current reservation of 20 percent of total funds for national use outside of state apportionments provides the federal government with the power to contract directly with public or private schools in a state which refuses to follow federal guidelines. Only 15 percent of total funds was used in this way in fiscal 1967, but the experience indicates how potent the unallocated reserve can be in winning adherence to federal policies (see Table 6–1).

The experimental and demonstration expenditures were made in addition to the earmarked E & D funds from Title I. The expenditures for health occupations were made at the specific direction of the White House. Concentrations of minority populations often seemed, from the national viewpoint, to merit higher priority than the general distribution of state allocations would allow. The $1 million to private schools represented a single contract to a national association of private business schools, awarded to circumvent the reluctance of public schools in a number of states to provide integrated classes in business subjects. The "critical occupations and upgrading of skills" category was a straightforward supplement for states that had exhausted their apportionment.

The states resent the reservation of 20 percent of the limited MDT budget for federal distribution and the implication that the "feds" have superior wisdom. In many cases, federal yielding to political pressure is clear, as is the ability to fund pre-

Table 6–1
Use of Unapportioned Account for Fiscal 1967

Project	Amount
	(*in millions of dollars*)
E & D-Related Institutional and On-the-Job Training	14.9
Training of Workers in Health Occupations	12.1
Training in Support of the Neighborhood Youth Corps	0.7
Aid to Special Groups (the urban and rural disadvantaged, Indians, the Spanish-speaking, migrant workers, etc.)	7.2
National Individual Referral to Private Schools for Institutional Training	1.0
Training for Critical Occupations and Upgrading of Skills	2.6
Concentrated Employment Program	2.5
Supplement to State Plans and State Apportionments	7.0
Total	48.0

mature as well as carefully thought out special programs. However, the potential of the provision for enforcing national policy is also readily demonstrable.

The right to recall uncommitted state allocations during the last half of the fiscal year prevents loss of funds because of failure of unaggressive states to use their full allocation. A reporting procedure allowing month-to-month monitoring of project status, enrollee characteristics, and employment experience will facilitate program monitoring without direct involvement of the federal government.

Labor Department officials remain concerned that a larger role for the states in MDT decision-making may reduce the program's flexibility. HEW officials are more inclined to permit such a role. With the trend to larger projects, the significance of the states' authority to approve projects costing less than $75,000 is declining. On the other hand, few states have chosen to use the funds set aside for these small, state-approved projects.

A useful experimental compromise would be the change in budgetary allocation formulas which has been suggested by the Division of Manpower Development and Training in the Office of Education. The primary concern is with an inherent bias in the program against small nonindustrial states, since the current formula is based in part upon labor force participation and covered employment. The proposal is to give each state a basic allocation of $1 million to use without federal project approval but within federal guidelines. This funding would materially increase the total training budgets of twelve states without significantly affecting the funds available to others. At the same time, it would provide experience with state-approved local projects without removal of federal review over the majority of projects. It would also allow states with skill centers to provide them with continuing support from the basic allocation.

There is nothing magic about the figure of $1 million, but the proposal appears to be a desirable step in the direction of reducing federal government involvement in administrative detail without reducing its primary responsibility for overall policy. Instead, the movement appears to be in the opposite direction. A decision in late 1967 removed authority for project approval from the regions, requiring that all projects be approved nationally by the Manpower Administrator. Ostensibly the decision was temporary, growing out of concern over accumulation of committed but unspent funds. Any substantial expansion of MDT is likely to demonstrate the inefficiency of this degree of centralization.

THE FUTURE OF MDTA

Given the proved success of the manpower development and training program, it is somewhat surprising that it has not been expanded more rapidly. The authorizing committees in Congress have given what was asked to them, and the appropriations committees have not been niggardly (Table 2–2). However, the program has been expanded time after time without a corresponding increase in funds to support the added services. The major constraint has come from the Budget Bureau, which partly reflects the Administration's wish to hold down total spending but which also reflects its doubts about the program's value and its awareness of the accumulation of unspent funds in state hands. Labor Department administrators have not pushed aggressively for increased funds, in part because an enlarged program would require a change in the federal-state relationship.

At the state and local levels the feeling seems to be almost universal that manpower training could be substantially increased with considerable profit and within the limits of available facilities. At the close of 1967 many state and local officials were concerned over the program's 1969 expiration date and advocated either early extension or endorsement of a permanent program to allow and encourage long-range planning. It was to supply a reassuring sign of permanence that Senators Clark and Prouty introduced a bill providing for a simple one-year extension. Budget restraints within the Executive Branch are such that expansion at this point appears unlikely. Those most familiar with MDTA appear to feel that its legislative authority is broad enough, and they advocate merely extending the program without change. In an election year, however, it is not unlikely that some embellishment may be advocated.

The breadth and permissiveness of the Manpower Development and Training Act is such that little can be added to the basic legislation. There is even danger that in their frustration at the failure of unemployment problems to "go away" after five years of attack, federal manpower administrators may divert MDTA funds from a soundly developing program to the pursuit of quick results. At the beginning of 1968 the involvement of private employers in concentrated attacks upon the problems of target areas in slums, though a useful weapon among others, posed such a threat because of overestimation of its possibilities.

A more useful area for legislative and administrative consideration is the melding of MDTA with other federal manpower programs. The underutilized skill centers offer training possibilities for enrollees in the Neighborhood Youth Corps, who at present receive little training of lasting value.[1] The Work Experience and Training program of the Economic Opportunity Act did use the centers in a few areas. It is unclear at present how much of the Job Corps' accomplishment is the product of its residential setting and how much that of training which could have been provided at less cost through skill centers. Using limited MDTA funds for basic education without coordinating the effort with other basic education programs in the community is a mistake. The continuing need for remedial skill training does not automatically justify setting up programs and facilities separate from preventive programs.

---

[1] Levitan, *Antipoverty Work and Training Efforts*, pp. 57–65.

Scattering OJT authority among vocational education institutions, MDT, and several components of EOA is also a questionable practice.

Of the continual need for a remedial training program, there appears to be little doubt. Vocational education and other occupational training is being expanded to meet more satisfactorily the needs of groups ranging from youths in school to employed adults. Greater emphasis should be placed on prevention of individual employment problems. With appropriate initial preparation, the future demands on MDT and other remedial programs could be reduced. Nevertheless, with an existing backlog of need and in an atmosphere of rising educational attainment and skill requirements, workers in need of remedial education and training directly related to current labor market demands will remain, and such training will be possible only if they are given financial support.

The funds available for training under Title II of MDTA could well be doubled within the capability of the present administrative system. Skill center facilities established with MDT funds are currently underutilized, while eligible trainees are available. The OJT program can also expand, with appropriate administrative controls to see that the added training slots go to disadvantaged persons whom employers would not otherwise hire.

Current research appropriations under the program are inadequate in the light of the need for expanding knowledge of the workings and failings of the labor market. The handling of experimental and demonstration projects argues against the current tendency toward contraction. The experience of the mobility projects supports proposals for a modest permanent program. Improvements could, of course, be made in the current use of both Title I and Title II funds. Difficult decisions must be made concerning objectives and training methods. But the expenditures have been and should continue to be profitable public investments.

Index

181